Diaper Days to Primary Grades

Strategies for Learning, Behavior, School Readiness and Life Skills

Judy Pierson
Child Wise Learning™

CHILD WISE LEARNING™ PUBLICATIONS

Copyright 2009 by Judy Pierson

Publisher: Child Wise Learning™ Publications
A Division of ChildWise Consulting Services, Inc.
2201 70th Avenue
Greeley, CO 80634

ISBN 978-0-615-30072-6

The content of this book is intended for general use only
and is not intended to diagnose or prescribe medical advice.

Actual case studies are given throughout this book.
Names and places have been omitted to protect privacy.

This book is dedicated to the children, adolescents,
parents and teachers who have taught me throughout my career.

"I can do anything I want. Nobody cares."
—TEEN STUDENT

"I don't need any books. I'm an F student."
—STUDENT IN A SCHOOL-BASED TEEN PARENT PROGRAM

"It's (students' behavior) much worse than it was five years ago."
—COMMENT FROM SEVERAL ELEMENTARY SCHOOL TEACHERS
IN THE EARLY 1990S

"Wait till they get the ones we have now."
—PRESCHOOL TEACHERS' RESPONSE
TO THE ELEMENTARY SCHOOL TEACHERS

"Help! A child just killed the guinea pig."
—CHILD CARE CENTER DIRECTOR

"(Child's name) was quiet today. Teacher not nice."
—23 MONTH-OLD-BOY ON CHILD CARE PROBATION FOR BEHAVIOR

"They're going to kick me out. They don't want me. Nobody wants me."
—FIVE-YEAR-OLD ANTICIPATING BEING EXPELLED
FROM ANOTHER PRESCHOOL

"Finally, someone who understands."
—WORKING MOTHER OF A THREE-YEAR-OLD
CLOSE TO GETTING EXPELLED FROM ANOTHER PRESCHOOL

"Thank you for helping me."
—RESPONSE FROM A SEVEN-YEAR-OLD WHO HAD BEEN DENIED
SCHOOL RECESS FOR SIX WEEKS AS A FORM OF PUNISHMENT

Contents

Charts

Introduction

This book is for parents, grandparents, teachers and other adults who have young children in their lives. It merges the new research of brain science and wellness with years of proven research on child development.

While there are times when any child can be a challenge, reports in recent years indicate an increasing number of children are entering school unprepared to learn and having difficulty regulating behavior. These difficulties are often the result of insufficient support that all young children need for optimal development.

The Role of Environments in Learning and Behavior

Environments affect children's learning, behavior and health. The environments of home, school and child care are all interrelated and play a role in a child's development. If a child is having difficulty at home, the issues will probably carry over to child care and school. Likewise, difficulties at school or child care will spill over into the home. Therefore, all aspects of a child's life must be considered when evaluating a child's needs. This means that parents, teachers and other involved adults must work together to meet the needs of an individual child. When caring adults take time to objectively observe a child's environment and make needed changes, problems with learning and behavior will usually improve.

The lives of children have been dramatically affected by societal changes. The trend of increased parental working hours plays a role in the number of hours children attend child care. Today, it is not unusual for infants to enter child care at four to six weeks of age. Time spent in non-parental care often exceed 50 or more hours per week. These are very long hours for young children, even when the care is high quality. Some studies have found an increase in behavior issues among children who spend long hours in child care. (National Institute of Child Health & Human Development, 2007)

In addition, the lives of school-aged children have been greatly impacted by school reform efforts. With limited funding and mandated standardized testing, schools have decreased or eliminated programs such as music and physical education classes. An increasing number of schools are eliminating recess (National Parent Teacher Association, 2006).

As a result, education for young children has dramatically changed. First, the curriculum has been moved down. Kindergarten now looks like the former first grade. Fewer kindergarten classrooms have activity centers. The old kindergarten curriculum is now taught in preschool. Second, children are required to sit more. This is a major challenge for most young children. Third, homework is now being assigned in kindergarten and first grade. This further decreases the possibility of active play after school.

Some primary-aged children attend child care programs before-and after-school. Others stay home alone before-and after- school while their parents work. Due to safety concerns, these children are often required to remain inside until their parents get home.

The Lost Childhood

By the time families get home, everyone is exhausted. It is time for homework, dinner and bedtime routines. It may too late for outside play. Some parents try to replace outdoor play with organized sports. As a result, imaginative outdoor play has given way to organized sports (Louv, 2005).While organized sports do have benefits, these benefits do not replace the benefits of free play (American Academy of Pediatrics, 2006).

While outside play has decreased, time watching TV and playing video games has increased. Many children spend more time with technology than interacting with adults. The effect of this on young children's developing brains has been a topic of much debate. Until further research is done, the American Academy of Pediatrics is recommending that children under the age of two not watch television.

While that debate continues, there is mounting evidence that lack of physical exercise, decreased sleep, increased stress and poor dietary habits are affecting children's physical and mental health. In addition, these factors also impact children's behavior and ability to learn.

Toxic Environments Create Bad Behaviors

When developmental needs are supported by the environment, children thrive. When development is not supported, children may have difficulty focusing, learning and meeting behavioral expectations. Children tell us through their behaviors when their needs are not being met.

There has been a dramatic increase in the number of young children being expelled from preschool and public education for behavior issues. The expulsion rate is actually higher among preschool children than among children in public schools (Gilliam, 2005).

Aggressive children can harm other children, parents and teachers. With one swipe of the hand, they can throw all the toys off the shelf and across the room. Other children may be afraid to be in the room with them.

Behavior Affects Learning

Few teachers are adequately trained to work with high-risk children. There are few counselors for children in preschool and elementary grades. Counselors who are available may not be adequately trained to work with young children. Most mental health professionals are trained to work with older children and adults.

When an aggressive child is not removed from the classroom, other parents and even teachers may demand action. Parents may threaten to move their children to another program. Teachers may threaten to quit their jobs. With teachers in high demand, directors will be more inclined to lose a child than a teacher. In addition, high-stakes testing in our public schools leaves little, if any, time for problem children. Problem behaviors can interfere with learning, not only for the difficult child but for the entire classroom.

Parents who are frequently called from work to pick-up their unruly children worry about losing their jobs. They may realize their children need help, but may not know were to find it or, they may not have the financial resources needed for professional assistance.

As children are expelled from one program to another, their self-esteem becomes more fragile and problems escalate. Without proper intervention, they are at an increased risk for school failure (Gilliam, 2005).

Aggressive children are not the only ones who are high risk for societal problems. Children who withdraw into their inner selves are also at high risk. They may sit in the corner staring into space or, they may roam around the room, crying inconsolably. As long as these children are not physically harming others, adults may tend to ignore them. However, the harm can be as damaging to their social and emotional development as the difficulties faced by aggressive children.

Solutions: Drugs Are Not The Answer

Meanwhile, the use of pharmaceutical drugs for behavior and concentration issues continues to increase (Tyre, 2005). The long term effects on children's developing brains are unknown (Kluger, 2003; National Scientific Council on the Developing Child, 2008). The U.S. Food and Drug Administration has ordered manufacturers to add label warnings about the increased risk of suicide to antidepressants used for children (U.S. FDA News, 2004).

The Research and Daily Practice Gap

All of this coincides with an explosion of research on child development, parenting, violence prevention and how children learn. We know more about what children need to become productive members of society than any other generation! However, there is a gap between research and daily practice in homes, child care and schools.

Our society seems to have lost touch with our children. We want quick-fix solutions. It is easier to blame a child than to repair our homes and educational institutions. It is easier to label children as dysfunctional and prescribe drugs than it is to try to understand them and correct our own behavior. We have forgotten that children are not miniature adults. Their minds and bodies are still developing. They respond, positively or negatively, to their environments. They get tired and stressed. They need play to help them de-stress and learn. They need positive guidance and interaction with adults – a need that cannot be fulfilled by any form of media. They need an educational system that functions the way they learn. Arranging our lives to support the needs of children is not a quick-fix solution. It is a long-term investment.

How to Use This Guide

It saddens me that common sense has disappeared – with teaching, parenting and society. Within your hands is over three decades of work that I created for my classes and workshops, via my extensive lesson plans for students – young and old. It's what I call Child Wise Learning ™. My personal goal for "Diaper Days to Primary Grades" is to bring common sense back to homes and classrooms.

This book is not intended to replace medical diagnosis or treatment. Rather, it should be used as a tool to bridge the gap between research and daily practice. Keep it on your desk or counter for quick reference. Use it as a tool to understand children and create environments that nurture development, decrease problem behaviors and improve learning.

PART 1

Growing and Learning for Today's Children

A basic knowledge of child development is a tool for understanding children.

I saw tomorrow look at me
From little children's eyes,
And thought how carefully we'd teach
If we were really wise.

—AUTHOR UNKNOWN

When young children explore the environment with their senses — touching, seeing, tasting, hearing and smelling — the brain develops networks. This is the foundation for lifelong learning.

CHAPTER 1

Learning:
It's a Process,
Not an Event

Throughout her pregnancy, the young mother softly talked and sang to her unborn child. As a newborn, the baby recognized his mother's voice. By three months of age, he cooed in response to his mother's voice. He now had enough muscle development to hold a baby rattle for a short time period. By six months of age, he began mimicking the sounds of his parent's language. He liked to play with toys on his floor mat. His muscle and nervous systems were now developed enough to support holding toys longer and rolling over. Sometimes he would get tired and over-stimulated from playing. As he cried, the mother would quietly talk or sing to him, with gentle rocking or massage. This soothed his nervous system and helped calm him. In a few months, he will begin to calm himself with a special toy or blanket. The process of learning to self-calm and interact with the environment will continue throughout childhood.

Learning is a process that starts before birth and continues throughout life. This process is affected by inherited genes, the quality of the prenatal environment, and interaction with the environment during childhood. As children explore the environment, they develop physically, intellectually, socially and emotionally.

The learning process requires communication between the body and the environment. This involves more than the brain. Children explore their environments through seeing, touching, smelling, hearing and tasting. Then the body's sensory system receives messages from the environment and delivers the messages to the brain. The sensory system depends on the nervous and muscular systems to operate efficiently.

The muscle and nervous systems begin to develop during the prenatal period and continue to mature throughout childhood, gradually giving children more ability to interact with their world. Developmental highlights, such as rolling over, sitting, crawling, standing, walking and running would not occur without the development of the nervous and muscular systems. For example, muscles and nerves must be developed around the bladder and kidneys before a child can be toilet trained. Likewise, mouth and throat muscles must develop before a child can learn to talk.

The brain begins developing during the first trimester of pregnancy, forming brain cells which will be used for learning. By the last trimester of pregnancy, the rate of brain development rapidly increases. The fetus has learned to suck his thumb and move in response to light and sounds outside the womb. The brain will continue developing rapidly throughout this last trimester until about the third year of life. Then brain growth will gradually slow, but will not be complete until after the second decade of life.

Biologically, learning occurs as a whole, not a part. The brain is not separate from the body, ready to be filled with information as the remaining parts sit idly by. It needs the body to send the information gathered by the senses of sight, smell, hearing, touch, taste and movement (Hannaford, 2005; Kranowitz, 2005). As the body gathers information from the environment, the information is sent to the brain for interpretation, processing and memory. The brain must decide whether the information is new or old. If the incoming information fits with existing information, it will be added to that neural circuit. If it is new information, a new circuit must be formed. These neural circuits, or learning pathways, are formed in early childhood and lay the foundation

> **Learning in Process**
>
> The toddler touched the new toy truck. He tasted and smelled it. He listened for sounds. Then he threw it. His father took the truck and gave him a soft ball that he could throw.
>
> At lunch time, he looked at the green peas. He threw some on the floor. Then he squished some between his fingers and rubbed them in his hair. He finally licked the peas on his fingers.
>
> This child was busy learning. He learned that toy trucks and green peas do not bounce the same way that balls bounce. He learned that green peas feel different in the hair than shampoo. He also learned that green peas and toy trucks taste and smell differently. Perhaps, after a few more tries, he will learn to eat the green peas.
>
> *Child Wise Learning*

for lifelong learning (National Scientific Council on the Developing, 2007).

Emotions are not separate from the body, either. The emotions are inter-related with learning (National Scientific Council on the Developing Child, 2004). Nerve networks are shared by emotions, thoughts and the body (Hannaford, 2005). Therefore, learning includes emotions and sensory input which travels back and forth between the brain and the body via the nervous and muscular systems. Movement activates the neural networks in the brain. **In other words, learning and memory will not occur without movement, emotion and sensory input.**

> **Learning in Process**
> The three-year-old colored a picture. She wanted to write words on her paper, but it was hard for her little fingers. Her brother said she was "scribbling." Her mother asked her to tell a story about her picture. While she told her story, the mother wrote the words under her picture.
> *Child Wise Learning*

This dance between biology and environmental interaction will continue throughout childhood. As the nervous and muscular systems develop, children will gain more ability to interact with the environment. Repeated experiences through environmental interaction form brain connections.

Children learn about their world through play by using sensory input, personal emotion and movement. As they explore their environments, they observe, wiggle, listen, make noise, touch and taste everything within reach. They must. This is how they learn. To deny them this, is to deny them brain connections for lifelong learning. The brain networks that are formed in early childhood are the foundation for future learning (National Scientific Council on the Developing Child, 2007).

Learning in Process
While playing with the blocks, the preschoolers made a tall tower. Then they made a row of blocks across the room. They counted how many blocks it took to go from one wall to the other. Perhaps they will be engineers someday.

Child Wise Learning

I tried to teach my child with books,

He gave me only puzzled looks.

I tried to teach my child with words,

They passed him by, often unheard.

Despairingly I turned aside,

'How shall I teach this child,' I cried.

Into my hands he put the key,

'Come,' he said, 'Play with me!'

—ANONYMOUS

CHAPTER 2

The Necessity of Play
is not a Myth

The grandmother telephoned about her granddaughter. The family read to her regularly, but she finished the first grade in the lowest reading group. They were concerned about second grade. Should they increase the reading time? I inquired about the granddaughter's activity level and suggested they keep reading while increasing activity. After a summer of added activity, the granddaughter was placed in the top reading group of her second grade classroom.

Families, communities and businesses are all concerned about school success. Teachers report that children are entering kindergarten unprepared to learn (Boyer, 1991). Families are concerned their children will be held back a grade. Businesses want their future employees to have problem-solving skills and the ability to cooperatively work with others. If children do not develop critical thinking skills, our society will be less innovative in the future (MacPherson, 2004; Perry, 2008). Rote memorization does not promote problem solving and reasoning (Hannaford, 2005). Play that engages creativity, imagination and physical activity is nature's tool for developing learning and life skills.

Productive Play – An Endangered Activity

Although numerous studies have documented the benefits of play, it has become an endangered activity for young children. Fewer children are playing outside, riding bicycles, climbing trees and exploring the great outdoors (Louv, 2005).

Children spend more time inside, due to family schedules and concerns for safety. More of this inside time is spent watching television and playing video games than engaging in pretend play. This requires little imagination and creativity. In fact, when children do try to play, they may simply imitate the media scenarios. This type of imitative play is nonproductive and may even be harmful to a child's developing brain. (American Academy of Pediatrics, 2006; Kieffer & Nicoll, 2005).

Activity has decreased in schools, as focus has shifted from developing the whole child – physically, socially, emotionally and intellectually – to educating the child's brain. Physical education, art, music and recess have been decreased or eliminated for more class time to meet federal mandates for standardized tests (National PTA, 2006; American Academy of Pediatrics, 2006).

This attempt to educate only the brain, while excluding other aspects of development, is now filtering down to younger children. Preschools and parents are feeling more pressure to have children ready for kindergarten. As a result, many preschools are spending more "seat time" on academics. Preschoolers are required to sit at tables to learn their ABCs. The use of flash cards, computer programs and video games for young children is increasing.

At the same time, we are experience skyrocketing rates of childhood obesity, attention deficit disorder (ADD), hyperactivity, depression and stress related illness. Children, through their behaviors and learning difficulties, are telling us that the current approach is not working.

Benefits of Play

Life skills are learned as children seek solutions to real life problems through play. For example, doll play can be used to help explain a new baby sibling or toilet training. A child who has been exposed to violence may reenact the violence through play in an effort to understand it. Play may also provide an outlet to needs that are not met in real life. For example, a child who is not a leader in real life can be a leader in a play scenario.

Self-regulation skills are learned through play. These skills include regulating emotions and behavior through self-discipline, planning and decision-making. This translates into better school success. Children who can regulate their behavior and learning are better students.

School readiness and academic performance improve when learning is play-based. Research indicates that young children learn best by actively exploring the environment with their senses. Play integrates the mind and body for learning and memory (Hannaford, 2005).

How Play Benefits Development

Play is an essential tool for helping children develop physically, emotionally, socially and intellectually. Play prepares children for their future roles as students, parents and citizens (Pierson, 1995).

Fantasy play increases the attention span, creativity, imagination and critical thinking skills (MacPherson, 2004; Pierson, 1995). Fantasy play requires both verbal and non-verbal communication. Children who play with other children learn to read body language. They learn that other people have feelings. They learn communication skills. The high level of verbal interaction improves language development and problem solving skills. These skills are needed to develop empathy. Children who engage in fantasy play are more creative and cooperative. They have more respect for others, more self-control and more self-confidence. Peer approval or disapproval quickly identifies what behavior is socially acceptable. Children learn to regulate their emotions and behavior through pretend play. This translates into increased attention and learning in the classroom (Spiegel, 2008).

Active play, such as swinging, riding toys and climbing, develops large muscles and balance. It improves blood flow to the brain, improving attention and increasing learning. Movement is essential for the development of the sensory system and the brain's neural networks.

The Play-Based Learning Classroom

The classroom was arranged with various learning centers. One was a housekeeping center, another was for block building. The reading and writing center was designed for either group or individual activities. Children who needed private time could crawl under a table or in an old bath tub with a book. Tables in the large group area could be used for art, snacks or lunch. An adjoining room was equipped with physical education materials and mats.

After group time, the children had free time for learning centers. As the children played in the learning centers, the teachers walked around the room with a clipboard and checklists, one page per child. As the teachers observed, they checked the skills acquired and noted which skills were lacking. They noticed one kindergartener who went from one learning center to another without playing. After determining that he was developmentally on a three-year-old level, they equipped the learning centers with some materials that were appropriate for three-year-olds. Then they made sure he stayed in the centers and played.

The teachers were aware of research linking motor skills with reading. They worked closely with the physical education teacher. When they observed students who were having difficulty learning to read, they alerted the P.E. teacher. Then the P.E. teacher helped those children with motor skills. After the motor skills were acquired, they could learn to read.

Children stayed in this classroom for both kindergarten and first grade. Those who needed additional skill development stayed for part of the second grade. As skills were developed, children moved up to the next level with their peers. By the middle of the second grade, all the children were on grade level or above.

Child Wise
Learning™

Activity benefits health through weight management and stress reduction. When weight and stress are managed, the risk of future disease including diabetes, heart disease, stroke and cancer is decreased.

Outside play has the additional benefit of sunshine. Ten to fifteen minutes of sunshine exposure without sunscreen activates vitamin D in the skin. Vitamin D benefits bones, muscles and the immune system (Holick, 2006).

The Role of Play in Development
Physical Development
  • Large and small motor skills
  • Coordination
  • Stress reduction
  • Brain circuits
  • Sensory system
Intellectual Development
  • Attention span
  • Creativity and imagination
  • Problem solving
  • Motivation for learning
Social and Emotional Development
  • Self-regulation of emotions and behavior
  • Communication skills
  • Socially acceptable behavior
  • Cooperation
  • Self-esteem

Child Wise Learning

Quiet play with puzzles, stringing beads, art activities, dressing dolls and block play develop small muscles and eye-hand coordination. Block building also develops problem solving and counting skills. These are necessary for math and science. If play includes more than one child, language and social skills will be included.

Play with sensory materials, such as water, sand and clay, helps children develop the sense of touch. Music increases language and listening skills, releases tension, and encourages self-awareness. Cooking involves language, math (measuring), and science (observing food changes).

Structured vs. Unstructured Play

Play can be structured or structured. Structured play includes physical education classes and organized sports. Unstructured play gives children free time to play what they want. Free play can be facilitated by adults through using questions during play and determining which play materials are available for children. Unstructured free play, such as recess, is more beneficial to development and resiliency than structured play, such as physical education classes. The American Academy of Pediatrics recommends that children have some free play that is unstructured and completely "child-driven" (American Academy of Pediatrics, 2006).

Daily Practices

Adults who are attuned to children's feelings and fatigue recognize over- and under-stimulation. Active play is alternated with quiet play throughout the day to give children time to process new learning and calm behavior. Children are given daily opportunities to explore their environments through sensory play and activities. Opportunities to develop and practice motor, language, thinking and emotional skills are included in daily schedules.

When Play is not Beneficial

While play is natural for most children, it can be challenge for others. These children will need adults to show them how to play (Wolfgang, 1977; Carlsson-Paige & Levin, 1990).

Non-players go from one activity to another without taking time to actually play. They may prefer to watch other children play, rather than participating themselves. They may not like to get their hands dirty. Adults need to show these children *how* to play. The following strategies are adapted from the works of Wolfgang, Carlsson-Paige and Levin.

Mirror play

- The child sits on the adult's lap with a mirror in front of them. They take turns making faces in the mirror.
- The child and adult look at each other. They take turns making faces at each other.
- The adult recites rhymes that include finger plays, while encouraging the child to imitate the words and movements.

Play with materials and objects

- The child sits on the adult's lap, while the adult finger paints.
- The child sits on the adult's lap with his hands on the adult's hands, while the adult finger paints.
- The child sits on the adult's lap, the child finger paints with one finger.
- The child finger paints without adult help. It may take several play sessions before the child obtains this skill. After finger painting is mastered, easel painting can be introduced.
- Repeat these steps, using sand.

Symbolic Play

- Adult and child make up a story, using miniature people and animal toys.
- Adult and child mold clay into objects and pretend they are real.
- Adult and child pretend toys are real. For example, a toy cup symbolizes a real cup.
- Adult and child draw pictures together, telling stories about their pictures.

Pretend Play

- Pair the non-player with a child who is a good player.
- Set the stage with props, such as housekeeping toys or space station toys.
- Role-model a play scene, while verbally explaining what is happening. For example, say, "I'm going to the space ship."
- Next, tell the child what to do.
  Give verbal directions. Example: "Pretend you see the space ship coming."
  Use verbal questions. Example: "Where is the space ship going?"
  Use nondirective statements. Example: "I see the astronauts."
- The adult becomes a non-participant when the child starts playing.

Non-productive players typically imitate scenes they have seen through the media. This is a low level of play that includes little or no creativity or thinking. Their play is often aggressive toward teachers and other children. Some of the same strategies that are used for non-players may also be effective for the non-productive player. Adding or changing props and using questions can alter the script (Carlsson-Paige & Levin, 1990). For example, a play scenario of aggressive soldiers can be altered by including props and questions about the soldiers' personal life. Do they write to their families? What do they eat? Where do they sleep?

If the intervention strategies listed here are not effective, further evaluation is needed. For more information, see Chapter 11.

Academic Skills	Play Activities For Pre-Academic Skills
Skills Needed for Self-Regulation • Space awareness • Self-discipline • Communication • Cooperation • Problem solving • Delayed gratification (patience)	• Fantasy, or pretend play, that lasts at least ten minutes with other players, includes imagination, communication, planning, decision-making and attention.
Skills Needed for Learning to Read • Ability to understand and use words • Visual discrimination of letters and numbers • Eye muscles developed for left and right movement • Auditory discrimination of letters and numbers • Focused attention	• Talking, singing, adult-child reading • Form letters and numbers with bodies • Write letters and numbers in sand, flour or cornmeal • Make letters and numbers with modeling clay • Active play with eye movement • Extended play that requires attention and concentration
Skills Needed for Learning to Write • Ability to understand symbolic meaning • Awareness of using print for communication • Development of small muscles in hands and fingers • Eye-hand coordination	• Using pretend toys that symbolize real life • Notice words in daily life, such as signs and food containers • Play that uses fingers and eye movement, such as art activities, modeling clay, building blocks and sorting objects according to size or color • Active play with eye movement
Skills Needed for Math and Science • Vocabulary – more, less, same • Categorizing • Ability to problem solve	• Play and movement activities that develop reading and writing pre-skills • Play that includes simple math and science, such as building blocks, sorting objects according to size or color and cooking • Extended play that requires attention and concentration • Music for increased brain development

©Judy M. Pierson, 2009 - ChildWise Consulting Services, Inc.

Newborn Characteristics

- Brain is ready to form learning pathways
- Personality is apparent at birth
- Senses are present
  - Can see within 12–14 inches
  - Recognizes sounds and voices heard before birth
  - Can distinguish mother's breast milk from others
  - Dislikes strong smells
  - Prefers viewing an actual human versus a picture

Human touch is as essential as milk for babies to survive.

Child Wise.
Learning

CHAPTER 3

The Process of Development:
Newborn to Eight-Years-Old

As the newborn was held by his mother, his father and grandfather talked, one on each side of the mother. The newborn slowly turned his head toward the familiar voice of the father.

A newborn enters the world totally dependent upon caregivers. The baby cannot turn over, talk or hold a spoon. Pain, hunger and cold can only be communicated by crying. Yet, this newborn is much more complex than is generally believed.

By birth, brain functions that control basic body functions are working. Automatic body functions, such as breathing and heart beat, are controlled by the brain. Basic motor movements are automatic, not voluntary. These movements are called reflexes. Rooting and sucking are examples of automatic reflexes.

Some basic senses are present at birth. People and objects that are close can be seen. Sounds that were heard before birth are recognized. Soft music may be especially soothing to the infant, if it was heard during the pre-natal period. Mother's milk can be identified by the smell.

Different and Alike

Each child enters the world as a **unique** individual with personality differences apparent in newborns. Every child grows and develops at an individual rate. For example, some babies walk at eight months, some at twelve months, and others later. While most begin saying simple words around the age of one, some will talk before the first birthday, others will wait until later.

> Shaking a baby can damage the brain stem, causing permanent disability and even death.
>
> *Child Wise Learning*

Yet, the process of development is the same for all children. Child development researchers have found many **similarities** in the way children grow and develop.

- **Growth is sequential. It follows a pattern.** Babies first learn to sit and then stand, before learning to walk.

- **Large muscles develop before smaller muscles.** For example, the muscles in the arms and legs develop before muscles in the fingers and toes.

- **Growth proceeds from the head down and the center out.** Babies can lift their heads before raising their chests. They lift their chests before learning to balance on their hands and knees.

- **Each developmental stage has unique characteristics.** Babies cry. Toddlers frequently say, "No." Three-year-olds like to tattle. Four-year-olds constantly ask, "Why?" School-aged-children like rules.

Developmental Areas

Child development contains categories that describe typical growth and development. Although society places more emphasis on cognitive or intellectual development, the categories are interrelated and equally important.

Physical Development – Refers to the rate of growth as measured by height, weight and motor skills, or muscle skills.

- **Gross motor development** refers to the development of skills involving the large muscles, such as walking, running and climbing.
- **Small motor development** refers to the development of skills involving small muscles. Examples of activities involving small motor development are holding a rattle or cup, coloring, writing, painting or stacking blocks.

Cognitive or Intellectual Development –
Refers to the child's ability to discover, process and use information.

Social and Emotional Development - The process of learning to interact with people, both peers and adults, is social development. Emotional development refers to the process of learning to recognize and manage emotions.

Speech and Language Development – Speech is the process of making sounds. Language development refers to the process of understanding and using words to express meaning.

Young Infants – The First Four Months
Physical Development
• Eyesight develops from a 12 inch range at birth to full range
• Sees in color by the fourth month
• Follows objects with eyes
• Learns to raise head and chest while lying on stomach
• Learns to roll over
• Grabs and holds small objects, but has difficulty maintaining hold

Speech and Language Development
• Coos
• Notices voices

Intellectual Development
• Laughs out loud around three months
• Recognizes familiar people
• Recognizes familiar sounds and smells

Social and Emotional Development
• Makes eye contact
• Smiles at others
• Beginning of sensorimotor play – the first stage of play
• Plays with fingers and toes
• Puts object in mouth
• Follows objects with eyes
• Likes toys that make noise
• Prefers seeing a real face rather than a picture of a face

Babies who are stressed may cry excessively, have cold hands and breathe rapidly.

Child Wise Learning

The Young Infant

Growing

The nervous and muscular systems will gradually develop enough to support some voluntary movement, such as turning over, cooing and holding small toys. This voluntary movement will then allow more interaction with the environment. The baby will learn how to use the senses – touch, taste, smell, hearing and seeing. Then these senses will be used to explore the environment. As the baby interacts with the environment, brain cells form connections for learning.

Eating

Nutrients from milk and interaction from the caregiver are necessary for proper growth and development. Cow's milk is not recommended for infants. Mother's milk, or infant formula, contains the right nutrients for the baby's rapid growth and development. Hypoallergenic formulas are available for babies who have a family history of food allergies.

Baby food is not recommended during this stage. The muscles for swallowing need a little more time for development.

A baby held during feeding receives more than nutrients. The human touch activates a growth hormone. This hormone facilitates the body's absorption of nutrients. Without human touch, nutrients are not absorbed and the baby fails to thrive. So, the process of caregiving is as critical for the healthy development of infants as food itself.

Playing

Young infants not only learn through their senses, they must learn how to organize and use the sensory system. At this stage, the infant prefers playing with an adult who will provide soft touch, gentle rocking, talking and singing. Crib mobiles and pictures posted on the wall by the crib will help stimulate the visual senses, but these cannot take the place of an adult. Research has shown that babies prefer to look at a real face rather than a picture of a face. Around two-and-a-half to three months of age, finger muscles will be developed enough to hold a small toy, such as a rattle, for short periods of time. Soft toys and other baby toys can be added at this time. Television and videos should not be used at this stage due to a possible interference with brain development.

> Young infants need a quick response to their cries. This teaches them to trust the adult. This trust will later be transferred to other relationships throughout life.
>
> *Child Wise Learning*

Behavior

Young infants cry frequently. Because muscles will not yet support talking, this is the only way they can communicate needs, such as pain, hunger, or fear. This is not misbehavior. Never shake a baby for crying or any other reason. Comfort the crying baby with soft music or talking and gentle rocking.

Sleep Patterns

Young infants need plenty of sleep to support their rapid growth. The number of total sleeping hours will gradually decrease, averaging about 15 of 24 hours around three months of age (National Sleep Foundation, 2004). Gentle rocking and soft music will help calm babies for sleeping.

Communication Skills

Daily routine care has many opportunities for quality interaction. Care tasks, such as feeding and diapering, provides an ideal time to talk, sing, and touch babies. For example, say, "Your diaper is wet. Let's get a dry diaper." before changing a baby's diaper. Then either continue talking or sing a song while changing the diaper. This helps soothe the baby and introduces the language. If baby sign language is being taught, show the sign while talking. For example, sign "diaper" while saying, "Your diaper is wet." This will help the baby learn words for objects. Do not, however, expect the baby to sign back to you at this stage. Finger muscles will need more development before this can happen.

Social-Emotional Skills

Babies can easily become over-stimulated. Adult interaction must carefully be balanced with the baby's need for quiet time. Alternating active time with quiet time will help minimize over-stimulation. Pay attention to the infant's mood. The baby will get fussy when he is ready for some quiet time. Gentle movement, such as rocking, can calm an over-stimulated child by soothing the nervous system.

During the first four months of life, the infant will form some basic trust or distrust with the primary caregiver. Crying is the only way young infants can express their needs. The adult must then determine what the baby needs – food, dry clothes, pain relief, touch, or comfort. When the adult consistently meets the baby's needs, the baby will learn to trust the adult. That trust can be then transferred to others. If the adult does not respond to the baby's cries, the baby will not learn to trust the adult. Trust is the first step in forming healthy relationships throughout life.

Ideally, there should be one consistent caregiver that the infant can learn to trust. In reality, many infants have multiple caregivers, including non-parental care. This can be a workable arrangement if the care is consistent and high quality. However, inconsistent care, such as frequent changes of caregivers in the child care arrangement, can interfere with the attachment process, setting the stage for a lifetime of distrustful relationships (Pierson, 1995).

Skills Young Infant Is Working On	Infant's Job	Adult's Job	Tools Needed
Learning to trust others (attachment)	• Cry to communicate needs	• Respond quickly to infant's needs	• Responsive adult, dry diapers, food, sleep, medical assistance as needed
Discovering senses	• Look, touch, taste, hear and smell objects	• Help infant hold and explore objects	• Infant toys with a variety of textures and sounds, pictures and mobiles posted close to crib
Develop motor skills	• Learn to hold head and chest erect • Learn to roll from back to side • Learn to hold small objects	• Provide time for gentle play	• Floor time with infant toys and an interacting adult
Language skills	• Learn to understand language • Learn to coo	• Read, talk and sing to infant	• Caring adult • Children's music • Books • Toys that talk

Skills Older Infant Is Working On	Infant's Job	Adult's Job	Tools Needed
Continuing to learn trust while learning to self-calm Language skills	• Communicate needs through crying, simple gestures or a few words. • Learn to soothe self with special blanket or toy.	• Continue responding to needs while encouraging infant to calm self with a special blanket or toy. • Encourage communication through gestures, such as sign language, and words.	• Responsive adult • Special blanket or toy • Soft music • Rocking chair • Simple signs or gestures for communication
Continuing to discover senses	• Explore everything within reach by seeing, touching, tasting, hearing and smelling.	• Provide appropriate infant toys. Guide infants in exploring objects. Put unsafe items out of reach. • Remove the crib mobile when the infant begins to reach it.	• Infant toys with a variety of colors, textures and sounds
Continuing to develop motor skills	• Learn to completely roll over, sit, crawl, stand and possibly walk. • Learn to pick up objects and self-feed finger foods.	• Get on the floor with the infant. Assist infant with sitting, crawling, standing, etc. • Encourage infant to hold objects and finger foods.	• Floor with pillow and infant toys • Provide finger foods small spoon, bowl and cup at about 8 or 9 months of age.

Older Infants – 5 to 12 Months
Physical Development
- Birth weight doubles by six months and triples by twelve months
- Completely rolls over
- Picks up small objects
- Learns to sit without assistance
- Learns to crawl
- Learns to pull to standing position, may begin to walk
- Begins to eat some solid foods
- Learns to hold own bottle or cup and self-feed finger foods

Speech and Language Development
- Understands and responds to familiar words, such as his own name, "Daddy," "Mama," and "Bye-bye."
- Babbles
- Imitates sounds
- Shakes head for yes and no
- May say a few words toward the end of this stage

Intellectual Development
- Responds to simple commands
- Begins to understand he is separate from his parents (individualism) and can make things happen (cause-and-effect)
- Likes to drop or throw objects and expects adults to retrieve them
- Realizes that people and object still exist even when not in sight

Social and Emotional Development
- Likes simple actions, such as pat-a-cake, peek-a-boo and waving bye-bye
- Imitates facial expressions and actions
- Shows preference for primary caregiver
- May experience anxiety when separated from primary caregiver (separation anxiety)
- Develops a fear of strangers around eight months (stranger anxiety)
- May become attached to a favorite blanket or toys
- Lifts hands to be picked up

Seek medical advice when an infant cries excessively or has difficulty eating.

ChildWise
Learning

The Older Infant

Growing

There will be great strides in large motor development at this stage, as the infant learns to sit, crawl, stand and possibly walk. Small motor skills will also improve. Around nine months of age, the baby will gain the ability to pick up small toys and finger foods with the forefinger and thumb.

Eating

Baby food can be introduced about six months of age. Introduce foods at least ten to fourteen days apart and avoid mixed foods. This will make it easier to identify possible food allergies.

Continue using mother's milk or baby formula at least through the first year. Cow's milk and honey should not be given to infants.

Playing

As mobility increases, the infant's view of the environment and response to adults will gradually change. There will be a strong need to explore by seeing, hearing, tasting, smelling and touching everything within reach. This is the first stage of play and is called sensorimotor play (Pierson, 1995). This is how young children learn and is essential to brain development. It will be essential to have a safe environment, with dangerous items out of reach.

The baby should have daily play time with an adult who will encourage exploration and skill development. This should be alternated with quite time to play alone.

Behavior

Older infants like to experiment with everything. They bang on their cups with a spoon and put their fingers in the food. They throw food and toys. Behavior is becoming more inconsistent. Remember that much of this behavior is a learning experiment. The ball bounces. Why doesn't the toy truck bounce? What is this new food on my plate? What does it taste like? How does it feel?

At this age, behavior can usually be redirected. When a child throws a toy that should not be thrown, take it away and replace it with a soft ball that can be thrown. When food is thrown from the high chair, sign and say, "All done." Then remove the child from the high chair and give him a toy that can be thrown.

Sleep Patterns

Older infants still need morning and afternoon naps. Morning naps may decrease toward the end of this stage. Use soft music, books, special stuffed animals or blankets to help infants *begin* to self-regulate their sleep patterns.

Communication Skills

Around the sixth month, the baby will start babbling, trying to mimic words in the parents' language. The baby notices non-verbal communication, such as gestures and emotions. Simple sign language for basic needs, such as diaper, food and drink, should be used with verbal words to teach communication. The infant will learn to recognize and use the simple signs before muscles are developed enough for verbal communication. Toward the end of this stage, vocal muscles will be developed enough to say a few simple words. A language-rich environment is necessary for the baby to continue learning communication. Baby books should be accessible and read to the infant. Talking, singing and reading to the baby help develop the language pathways in the brain.

Social-Emotional Skills

Separation and stranger anxiety will peak during this stage. Some will experience separation anxiety when parents leave them in another person's care. Others may experience anxiety when around strangers. This is normal development and typically is not a cause for concern. The ability to recognize and display emotions and anger will increase, but the ability to self-calm and communicate will be lacking. A special toy or blanket with some quiet time will help, but a responsive adult who can calm the infant is still essential. This is a continuation of forming trust for future relationships.

Frequently confining infants and young toddlers in cribs, playpens, swings and seats can interfere with brain growth and development. The results can be permanent (Carnegie Corporation, 1994). *Child Wise Learning*

The Young Toddler – 12 to 24 Months
Physical Development
- Growth is slower – appetite decreases
- Walks without assistance
- Attempts to run
- Crawls downstairs backwards on hands and knees
- Releases objects voluntarily
- Learns to eat with spoon
- Turns book pages
- Scribbles with crayons
- Stacks two to four objects

Speech and Language Development
- Understands "yes" and "no"
- Points to objects or people when asked
- Speaks five to fifty words
- Begins using two-word sentences
- Likes nursery rhymes

Intellectual Development
- Can follow simple directions
- Names some objects
- Makes a small block tower
- Enjoys books and pictures
- Demonstrates understanding of relationships, such as spoon and bowl
- Puts items in container and dumps them out

Social and Emotional Development
- Plays alone
- Less afraid of strangers
- Will help clean up toys with adult assistance
- Enjoys mirror play and naming body parts
- Temper tantrums becoming more frequent
- Curious
- May show empathy when another child cries

The Young Toddler
Growing

By the first birthday, the birth weight has tripled. If walking has not already occurred, it should be attained early in this stage. The toddler's head will be large in proportion to the rest of the body. Because of this, together with immature development of leg muscles, the toddler will walk with an unsteady motion. This is why they are called "toddlers."

Growth will slow dramatically in this stage. The body will need to catch up with the size of the head. Motor and language skills will need to be refined.

Eating

If the toddler is not already self-feeding, it should occur early in this stage. The finger muscles will now be developed enough to use a spoon, but not with ease. Finger foods will still be preferred. Appetites will decrease due to the slowed growth. Offering nutritious foods at snack time helps balance the lighter eating at mealtimes.

Playing

Young toddlers will continue to explore the environment with their senses. This sensorimotor play will continue throughout the preschool years. Around 18 to 20 months of age, play will advance to include symbolic play. In symbolic play, toy objects represent real objects. For example, a toy cup may represent a cup of coffee or tea (Pierson, 1995).

Young toddlers like to carry objects from one place to another. They like toys that stack or hold smaller toys. Toys that are pushed and pulled are popular with this age. Large motor activities, such as running and safe climbing, will help further develop the large muscles. Exploring and running are essential tools for brain development and should be part of the daily routine. Fine motor activities, such as coloring and block play, should be provided to further develop the small muscles in the fingers.

> A child who does not talk by the age of 18 months should be evaluated by a speech pathologist and an audiologist.
>
> *Child Wise Learning*

Most play at this stage is individual or alone play. Young toddlers may engage in parallel play, playing next to others, but not actually playing together.

Behavior

Temper tantrums will gradually become more frequent. Toddlers who had their needs met during infancy generally have fewer tantrums. The ability to communicate needs also helps decrease tantrums. Toddlers will observe and, at least part-time, try to imitate the behavior of others – parents, grandparents, teachers and other children. Children can be taught to regulate their behavior, but it will take time.

Sleep Patterns

Morning naps will be eliminated sometime between 12 and 18 months of age. Afternoon naps will still be needed. A regular routine of reading before naps and nighttime will help children settle down. Soft toys and music may help children learn to self-calm and regulate sleep.

Communication

Toddlers are still learning about their senses and trying to match words with their experiences. Adults can help in this process by providing experiences with different colors, sounds, textures, taste and smells. Make comments, such as, "This is soft" or "Here is the red car." Continue giving simple baby signs with the verbal words.

Social-Emotional Skills

Crying when another child cries or a parent leaves the room can be nerve-wracking for adults. However, at this stage, these are good signs. When a child cries because another child is crying, it is a sign of empathy. It means the child recognizes the sad feelings of the first child. This is an important part of healthy relationships. Adults can help by talking about feelings. For example, "He's crying because he is sad." Crying for a short time when a parent leaves is a good sign of parent-child attachment, or trust. This is a normal part of development and seldom is a cause for concern.

Skills Toddler Is Working On	Toddler's Job	Adult's Job	Tools Needed
Continuing to learn trust, how to self-calm and how to communicate needs	• Communicate needs through simple gestures or words. • Learn to soothe self with special blanket or toy.	• Continue responding to needs while encouraging toddler to calm self and express needs. • Encourage communication through gestures, sign language, and words.	• Responsive adult • Special blanket or toy • Soft music • Rocking chair • Simple signs or gestures for communication • Books
Learning to be an individual separate from parents	• Explore environment while staying close and periodically touching base with primary caregiver	• Allow exploration within a safe environment	• Responsive adult • Safe environment
Empathy for others	• Learn to read facial cues of others, such as happy and sad expressions. • Learn to recognize that others have feelings.	• Talk about feelings: "Are you happy?" "He's crying because he is sad."	• Responsive adult • Books about feelings • Pictures of various facial expressions

Skills Toddler Is Working On	Toddler's Job	Adult's Job	Tools Needed
Large and small motor skills	• Walk, run, climb, explore environment • Improve holding and grasping skills	• Provide a safe and supervised environment where toddler can practice skills	• Toys for large motor development, such as riding toys, balls and small climbing toys or pillows • Toys for small motor development, such as blocks, cars, dolls, dishes and crayons
Independence	• Feed self • Learn to dress and undress • Learn to use the toilet	• Encourage self-help in feeding, dressing, toileting and picking up toys	• Daily routines of eating, dressing, toileting and cleaning-up
Continuing sensori-motor play Beginning of symbolic play	• Continue exploring with senses • Learn to pretend that toys are real things	• Model how to pretend with toys	• Dolls, stuffed animals, dishes and other housekeeping toys, cars, trains, riding toys

The Older Toddler – 24 to 36 Months
Physical Development
• Runs with confidence
• Carries objects while walking
• Can draw a vertical line
• Will probably achieve toilet training
• Likes to fasten and unfasten clothes
• Throws a large ball underhanded

Speech and Language Development
• Speaks 50 or more words
• Asks "What's that?" and "Who's that?"
• Likes stories and songs
• Refers to self as "Me" or "I"
• Uses two-to-three word sentences
• Frequently says "No," "Mine," and "Do it myself."

Intellectual Development
• Will search for a hidden object
• Pretends that toys are real objects (symbolic play)

Social and Emotional Development
• Plays beside other children, often without interacting
• More curious
• Temper tantrums are common
• Likes to be center of attention
• Difficulty making choices
• Shows empathy
• Learning to be independent with dressing, feeding and toileting

The Terrific Two-Year-Old

Growing

By the age of two, the body and head are in better proportions. This makes it easier to run, carry objects and play ball. Small motor skills have improved enough to fasten and unfasten clothes.

Toilet training may be achieved during this stage. The nerves and muscles around the bladder must be developed before the child can be toilet trained. As a general rule, the child should be physically capable of keeping a diaper dry for at least two hours before training is started. If more than one caregiver is involved, all must be committed to the same training process.

Eating

Eating patterns will become inconsistent. The older toddler may eat little for several days and then eat well for a while. This can be frustrating for adults who are concerned about adequate nutrients for development. However, as long the child is growing properly, this should not be a concern. Since growth has slowed, less food is needed. Healthy snacks can balance the irregular mealtime eating.

Playing

Sensorimotor and symbolic play will continue during this stage. Symbolic play will become more elaborate as language skills improve. Now, pretending to drink from a cup may include verbal details about the entire pretend meal.

Active play will continue as the older toddler works to refine large motor skills. Small motor activities, such as coloring and block building, will become more interesting as the child gains more control of finger muscles.

Behavior

"No. Do it myself." This is a common statement of twos. They want to be independent, although they still need help. They want to make their own choices, but have difficulty doing so. They have little control over their lives, except for toilet training and eating. As a result, temper tantrums peak during this stage.

The frequency and intensity of tantrums will vary from one child to another. Children who have had responsive caregivers during infancy tend to have fewer tantrums. Those who have acquired enough communication skills to express their needs may also have fewer tantrums. Nevertheless, tantrums will still occur at this stage. These will decrease after language, self-help and self-calming skills improve.

Letting the child toilet train a doll that wets can help teach the toilet training process. *Child Wise Learning*

Tantrums will often stop when they are ignored. If this doesn't work or if the tantrum occurs in a public place, carry the child to a quiet place and hold him until he calms down. Say, "I will hold you until you feel better." When the child calms enough to listen, remind him to, "Use your words."

Sleep Patterns

Older toddlers often think they are too busy for sleep. However, sleep is essential to help regulate behavior and the immune system. Afternoon naps should still be taken.

Children should now be able to self-calm and go to sleep after hearing a story. Books, special toys and blankets on the bed can help children calm. It is appropriate to expect a quiet time of 30 to 60 minutes even if the child doesn't take a nap.

Communication

Language skills now include two or more words per sentence.
Most two-year-olds can speak well enough to tell adults how they feel and what they want. However, they don't always remember to do this. They need to be reminded to use their words.

Social-Emotional Skills

The two-year-old wants to be independent. Adults should encourage this. If foods are not too hot, let children spoon the food from the bowl onto their plates. Lay their clothes on the floor and encourage them to dress themselves. Children who feel they have some control will have fewer power issues.

The Transitioning Three-Year-Old – From Toddlerhood to Preschool
Physical Development
- Baby fat is gone, neck is now apparent
- Alternates feet when walking up and down stairs
- Can balance and hop on one foot
- May jump in place
- May walk on toes
- Can peddle a tricycle
- Can kick a ball
- Draws circles, vertical and horizontal lines
- Probably toilet trained – may still have accidents
- Holds crayons with a tripod grasp

Speech and Language Development
- Vocabulary of 300 or more words
- Likes to show off new words by singing, telling stories and tattling
- Speaks sentences with 3 or more words

Intellectual Development
- Increased attention span
- Recognizes a square, rectangle and triangle
- Can sort objects according to color or shape
- Has a limited understanding of time

Social and Emotional Development
- Play expands from symbolic to imaginative play
- Nightmares and fears are common
- May have an imaginary friend
- Likes attention – may tattle to get it

The Transitioning Three-Year-Old

Growing

The three-year-old is in the process of transitioning from toddler to the preschool stage. A young three-year-old will look more like a two-year-old. An older three will have more four-year-old characteristics.

The baby fat begins to disappear, making the neck appear longer. Large and small motor skills will dramatically improve during this stage. This will be noticeable in regular daily activities, such as walking, eating, playing and dressing. Walking up and down the stairs will become easier as the child learns to alternate feet (Allen & Marotz, 1994).

If toilet training was not accomplished during the toddler stage, it will probably be during this stage of development. The muscles and nerves around the bladder should be stronger. However, some help will still be needed and occasional toileting accidents will still occur.

Eating

Appetite will be more regular now, but there will still be off days when less food is eaten. Continue supplementing meals with nutritious snacks. Eating with a spoon will be easier. Drinking from a cup without a lid will also be easier, but spills will still occasionally occur. Small cups will be easier for little hands.

Playing

Sensorimotor and symbolic play will continue. These will gradually expand to social dramatic play. This is a higher level of play than imitative symbolic play. Social dramatic, or imaginative play, still includes toys that symbolize real objects but, it includes more imagination and verbal exchanges among players (Pierson, 1995). One example of social dramatic play is playing house, with players pretending to be different members of the family.

> Learning to make choices is an important part of self-regulation. It is a skill that must be learned.   *Child Wise Learning*

Large muscles will develop enough to ride a tricycle or hop on one foot. Fine motor skills will improve the ability to draw, color and sort small objects according to size and color. It will still be easier to draw straight lines than shapes, such as squares and rectangles.

Behavior

Nightmares, fears and imaginary playmates may begin at this stage and will probably continue into the next stage. The child's ability to self-calm is still not complete. Adult guidance will still be needed to calm fears. Tantrums should be fewer, but may still occur occasionally.

Sleep Patterns

Hours of sleep will gradually decrease during this stage. Afternoon quiet times should still be part of the daily routine. Most children still take naps during this stage, but they may be shorter.

Bedtime may become a struggle. Having a bedtime routine that includes reading can be helpful. Reading books that address childhood fears may be useful. A special blanket, soft toys and calming music can help calm anxious children. Adult comfort and reassurance will still be needed.

Communication

By now, vocabulary has increased significantly. The process of learning *how* to use the words will continue throughout early childhood. The three-year-old loves to show off all the new words. One way to do this is by tattling. Making a big issue of this can actually increase the behavior. Decrease the attention on the tattling by saying, "Thank you," then focus attention on the positive use of words by asking the child to sing a song or tell a story. The story will likely include some confusion of the use of words and sequence of time events. For example, statements such as, "I go-ed to the store" or "I didn't go to school tomorrow" are common at this stage.

Social-Emotional Skills

Simple choices should be introduced at this stage. Choices should be age-appropriate. Never give choices that a child cannot accomplish or that could be harmful. Instead, give choices for things the child can already do and that are a part of the regular routines. For example, "Do you want to brush your teeth first? Or take your bath first?"

The three-year-old will continue to work on self-help and self-calming skills. Dressing and undressing will become easier as the small muscles in the fingers develop. This will be a big plus as toileting skills are accomplished. The three-year-old can pour a cup of water from a small pitcher. Snacks and art supplies on low shelves can be reached without adult help. Behavior, eating and sleeping are becoming better regulated.

Adult guidance is still needed, especially with emotions.

Skills 3s and 4s are Working On	Child's Job	Adult's Job	Tools Needed
Continuing to learn how to trust and self-calm	• Learn to plan actions • Expand tools for self-calming from security blankets and special toys to other items, such as books and music	• Continue to be available to child • Guide efforts to understand cause-and-effect of behavior • Encourage self-calming	• Responsive adult • Special blanket or toy • Add other tools for self-calming, such as books, music, or puzzles
Continuing to learn about emotions and empathy	• Learn to read facial cues of others, such as happy and sad expressions • Learn to recognize that other people have feelings • Learn to verbally express own emotions	• Talk about feelings: "Are you happy?" "He's crying because he is sad."	• Responsive adult • Books about feelings • Pictures of various facial expressions • Chart, spin wheel or stickers with various facial expressions used to help child identify own feelings
Language and pre-reading skills	• Learn to form new words into sentences that can be understood by others • Learn to recognize that letters make words	• Engage child in communication through talking, singing and reading • Help child read simple words, such as traffic and store signs	• Responsive adult • Books, music, finger plays, simple games

©Judy M. Pierson, 2009 - ChildWise Consulting Services, Inc.

Skills 3s and 4s Are Working On	Child's Job	Adult's Job	Tools Needed
Large and small motor skills Eye-hand coordination	• Develop large and small motor skills • Improve eye-hand coordination for future reading and writing skills	• Provide a safe and supervised environment where motor skills can be safely practiced	• Active play for large motor skills, such as climbing equipment, swings, balance beams, riding toys and balls • Quiet play for small motor skills, such as blocks, stringing beads, and art activities
Independence	• Learn to feed, bathe and dress self • Learn to tend to own toileting needs • Learn to help with simple chores, such as picking up toys and helping clear table after eating	• Encourage self-help skills	• Daily routines of eating, dressing, toileting and cleaning-up
Symbolic or imitative play continues Pretend or Fantasy play begins	• Continue exploring with senses and engaging in symbolic play • Learn to engage in pretend play with a group of children	• Provide various play activities that involve using the senses, such as cooking and art activities • Provide play materials for pretend play and show children how to pretend	• Art supplies, water, sand, cooking activities • Housekeeping toys, such as dolls and dishes • Blocks with props, such as small cars

The Four-Year-Old
Physical Development
• Skips
• Can hop on one foot
• Walks on a balance beam
• Crosses legs when sitting on floor
• Cuts on a line with child scissors

Speech and Language Development
• Recites and sings simple songs and rhymes
• Correct use of past tense, such as "I went to the store."
• Most sounds are clear

Intellectual Development
• Increased attention span
• Understand sequence of daily activities
• Understands some concepts, such as big vs. little
• Can count some objects
• Can rote count to 20 or more
• May read some words

Social and Emotional Development
• Boastful
• Bossy
• Engages in name calling
• May still have an imaginary playmate
• May still have fears
• May have some understanding of taking turns
• Engages in dramatic play with a group of children

The Inquisitive Four-Year-Old

Growing

With improved large motor skills, the four-year-old will skip, swing, walk on a balance beam and ride a bike with training wheels (Allen & Marotz, 1994). Active outdoor play should be provided regularly so these skills can be refined. Small motor skills are gradually improving. The four will learn to cut on a line with child scissors and string beads. Coloring will become more precise. Block building becomes more elaborate.

Self-help skills have improved. Toilet training, dressing and undressing probably have been achieved.

Eating

Appetite will fluctuate with growth and activities. Preschoolers prefer familiar foods, generally plain and unmixed foods. New foods may need to be introduced several times over a ten-to-fifteen-week time period before the preschooler will like it. Serve new foods with familiar foods. Let children help with simple food preparation.

Playing

Play becomes more imaginative and can include several players. A single play scene might include several scenarios, such as housekeeping, a fire station and a school.

The daily schedule should include time for active and quiet play. Active play will help refine large motor skills. Quiet play, such as puzzles and crafts, will help refine the small motor skills.

Behavior

Nightmares, fears and imaginary playmates may still be apparent at this stage. Adult comfort, security blankets and special toys may still be needed to help the child calm.

The four-year-old is very inquisitive, wanting to know how everything works. At times, it may seem the only word the four-year-old knows is, "Why?"

Sleep Patterns

Afternoon naps will vary at this stage, depending largely on schedules and how much sleep is received at night. Some children will not take any naps. Others may need at least an occasional nap. It is still appropriate to expect a quiet time for children who do not nap. Bedtime routines and security blankets are still needed at this age.

Quarrels over toys can be used to teach conflict resolution skills. Who had the toy first? What can the other child do while waiting for a turn?

Child Wise Learning

Communication

Language now includes using prepositions, such as on, in and under (Allen & Marotz, 1994). There is some understanding of yesterday, today and tomorrow. Past and present tense are used correctly. Sentences include four or more words. The four-year-old is comfortable with the use of words and does not hesitate to be boastful, bossy or call others names.

Social-Emotional Skills

The four-year-old has refined many skills. The four should have learned to trust the primary caregiver. This trust can now be transferred to others. The child will now be comfortable exploring and interacting with others. There will be little or no anxiety from brief separation from parents or meeting strangers.

The four is now bridging thoughts and emotions with action. Much to the dismay of adults, it seems that every other word of a four-year-old is, "Why?" Yet, asking questions, playing and participating in sensory activities are critical for continued brain development and school readiness.

Self-calming skills have improved, but some adult help will still be needed. The four is still learning how to recognize, understand and express emotions. There is some understanding of taking turns, but adults are needed to show *how* to take turns and share.

The Five-to-Seven-Year-Old – Transitioning From Preschool to Elementary School

Physical Development
- Growth spurts – and appetites – alternate with slow growth
- Can walk backward
- Can walk on a balance beam
- Skips
- Enjoys acrobatics
- Learns to ride a two-wheel bike
- Colors precisely and for longer time periods
- Copies shapes and letters
- Learns to tie shoes

Speech and Language Development
- Learns several new words every day
- Likes to tell stories
- Enjoys jokes and riddles with humor
- Talks constantly
- Likes to use "dirty" words
- Strong interest in written words

Intellectual Development
- Beginning to think somewhat logically
- Understands the concept of less and more
- Can consider other people's point of view
- May complete some math without objects to count
- Achieves an understanding of the difference between fantasy and reality
- Wants to know where babies come from
- Has difficulty understanding winning and losing
- Works in spurts
- Enjoys collecting and sorting items by type, color, shape and size
- Understands the purpose of a calendar
- Learns to tell time

Social and Emotional Development
- Usually has one or two special friends
- Prefers to play with own age group
- Protective of younger children
- Still needs adult comfort, but may not seek it
- Likes rules and expects fairness
- May become fearful of losing a parent
- Peer group is becoming more important

The Five-to-Seven-Year-Old

Growing

A major change in development occurs between the ages of five and seven. This has been referred to as "The five to seven-year shift" (Carnegie Corporation, 1996).

Large motor skills will develop enough to ride a bicycle and play organized sports. Small motor activities, such as writing and tying shoes, will become easier as muscles in the fingers develop.

There will be a large jump in thinking abilities as the brain continues to develop and begins to fine tune what it has learned. Children will begin to think more logically. This shift will be seen in every aspect of daily life, including learning and relationships.

Eating

Appetites will continue to fluctuate with growth patterns. There still may be periods of food jags and a resistance to new foods. Remember that children are more likely to eat foods that they helped prepare. As small motor and reading skills improve, it becomes easier for children to read children's cookbooks and prepare simple snacks and meals.

Playing

As motor skills become more refined, play skills will also change dramatically. Play groups will change from several children to one or two best friends. While some play will still be imaginative or dramatic play, there will be a shift to games with rules. Board games, organized sports and video games will be popular with this age group. If the games don't already have rules, the children will make up rules and expect everyone to follow them. Interest in drawing, writing, collecting and sorting items will increase. This is the perfect time to introduce hobbies, such as coin or rock collecting.

Many children will experience a strong emphasis on school readiness the year before starting kindergarten. Others will not have sufficient school-readiness experiences. All will begin their primary education during this stage. Entry into formal education usually requires more seat time. While the emphasis will be on fine motor and intellectual skills, there will still be a strong need for active time. Balancing the seat time with active time will play a major role in physical and mental health. Large motor activities, such as running and climbing will continue to be essential for optimal health and development.

Behavior

Emotions will become more stable during this stage. While physical disputes may still occur, disagreements will now include verbal attacks. With adult guidance, children can learn to settle disputes through communication.

Children in this stage are free with their opinions and may appear to be "know-it-alls." They will complain of unfair treatment and be sensitive to criticism. They will demand rules and fairness.

Sleep Patterns

Naps will probably be few or non-existent at this stage. Adequate night-time sleep will be essential. Some children will still enjoy listening to a bedtime story. Others may prefer to read to themselves.

Communication Skills

There will be a dramatic increase in language skills. Children of this stage enjoy telling stories, jokes and riddles. Some will practice their new language skills by using "dirty" words.

Social-Emotional Skills

Children begin to think more logically and understand that others may think different than they do. Understanding the difference between fantasy and reality should occur during this stage. There may be questions about where babies come from and what happens when someone dies. If that happens, short, age-appropriate answers should be given. If the child's curiosity is not satisfied, he will ask more questions.

Skills 5s, 6s, and 7s are Working On	Child's Job	Adult's Job	Tools Needed
Reasoning skills change from being self-centered to more logical thinking	• Learn to problem solve, using real objects • Learn to consider others' view point • Learn to understand the difference between fantasy and reality	• Provide opportunities to problem solve with objects • Continue talking about feelings • Place a strong emphasis on conflict resolution skills • Talk about the difference between fantasy and reality • Talk about death as opportunities arise, such as a dead animal • Provide simple answers to child's questions about sexual issues	• Math and science projects with real objects • Discuss issues about real vs. fantasy, others' point of view, feelings and death as topics occur in daily experiences through books, videos, television and play
Improve language skills	• Practice more elaborate use of language through telling stories and jokes • Learn to communicate through writing	• Provide opportunities to tell and write stories • Provide appropriate jokes and tongue twisters	• Books • Pencil and paper • Opportunities to verbally communicate • Introduce a second language

Skills 5s, 6s, and 7s are Working On	Child's Job	Adult's Job	Tools Needed
Improve motor skills More emphasis on organized games and sports vs. fantasy play Have a special friend	• Engage in sports and games with rules • Learn to play by rules • Learn to play with one or two special friends vs. a large group	• Provide supervised opportunities for games and sports with rules • Continue offering child time alone • Respect child's need to play with only one or two special friends • Introduce hobbies	• Organized games and sports • Introduce lessons, such as gymnastics or music (don't over-schedule – limit to one at a time) • Tools for hobbies or collections, such as stamp or coin collections

©Judy M. Pierson, 2009 - ChildWise Consulting Services, Inc.

The Eight-Year-Old
Physical Development
- Growth spurts continue to alternate with periods of slow growth
- Large motor skills are more complex
- Small motor skills are more refined

Speech and Language Development
- Ability to use words for more complex communication
- Tells stories with plots
- Increased ability to communicate through writing

Intellectual Development
- Understands cause-and-effect
- Increased ability to think logically
- Understands that others have feelings
- Has a longer attention span
- Understands the difference between fantasy and reality

Social and Emotional Development
- Peer group is increasingly important
- Reacts to peer-group approval and disapproval
- Accepts some responsibility for personal actions
- Probably has a best friend
- Enjoys organized games and sports

The Eight-Year-Old

By the age of eight, a child has made great strides in all areas of development. Physical growth will continue to alternate with slow and rapid periods. With the advancement of large motor skills, there is a greater desire to participate in organized games and sports. Small motor skills will continue to improve, making writing and drawing more enjoyable.

The dramatic increase in brain development has improved reasoning skills, learning, and communication. Thought processes are more complex, making it is easier to understand other people's opinions.

 Social skills are also changing rapidly. The pressure of peer approval and disapproval is increasing. This will continue to increase throughout the remainder of childhood and adolescence. The child who has developed a strong foundation in early childhood will weather the storms of pre-adolescence and adolescence better than the child who has had little support in the early years.

PART 2

Balanced Living
For Home and School

Balanced living improves learning and behavior.

There is more to life than
increasing it's speed.

—GANDHI

Physical Symptoms of Stress

- Increased Heart Rate
- Rapid Breathing
- Cold Hands
- Tight Muscles
- Upset Stomach
- Headache
- Weight Gain
- Impaired Immune System
- Learning & Memory Impairment

Behavioral Symptoms of Childhood Stress

- Inconsolably Crying
- Withdrawal
- Aggression

CHAPTER 4

Stressed Culture: Stressed Children

The preschool room was chaotic as the children were instructed to clean up at the end of the day. The regular classroom teacher was not in the room. Other teachers were entering and leaving the classroom. One teacher entered and screamed at a boy to get in his chair. Without taking his eyes off her, he backed into the chair. As soon as the teacher walked out of the room, the boy stood up and with one swipe of his hand threw the toys from the shelf and across the room.

In another classroom, the toddlers were crying loudly and inconsolably as the stressed teachers attempted to meet all their needs. One little boy retreated to a corner with his blanket and thumb. He stared into space, seemly unaware of the chaos around him.

The behaviors of these children were completely different. The preschool boy was aggressive. One toddler was passive, withdrawing into his inner world. The other toddlers were crying. Yet, the root cause of their behaviors was the same. They were all responding to the stress in their environments.

Hurried stress has become part of the American culture. Adults are hurrying to complete their over-scheduled tasks. Sleep is decreased. Meals are skipped. Family time has been decreased. Work is taken along on vacation. Most of the adults in the lives of today's children are stressed. Stress is accepted as normal for adults in our society.

Common Childhood Stressors
• New Experiences
• Transitions
• Inconsistent Care
• Insufficient Sleep
• Imbalanced Diet
• Illness
• Stressful Environments

Child Wise Learning™

Our society, however, is not supportive of the fact that children have stress, too. We forget that adult stress can cause stress in children. We expect children to be immune to stress. Yet, researchers have found that not only do children have stress, their symptoms can be as severe as the symptoms experienced by adults.

In fact, stress can have a negative impact on the physical and behavioral health of both children and adults. It affects the immune system, respiratory and cardiovascular systems (National Institute of Health, 2008; Middlebrooks &Audage, 2008). It can interfere with sleep and eating patterns. It affects learning and memory (Cooke, 2008)

The impact of prolonged chronic stress in young children is a major concern. Long-term chronic stress is toxic to young developing brains. It can interfere with the formation of connections between brain cells, decreasing communication among brain cells. Chronic childhood stress can result in a smaller brain with impaired brain chemicals, permanently affecting learning and behavior (Cooke, 2008).

The response to stress will vary with individual children. How a child responds to stress depends on the individual child's perception of the problem, the amount of stress, and what supports are available from family and community (Pierson, 1994). One child may

> **Extreme stress in the early years can cause permanent brain damage.**
>
> *Child Wise Learning*

exhibit only one or two symptoms, while another child may exhibit several symptoms. Children who have experienced prolonged periods of chronic stress, such as child abuse, have more difficulty coping with stress (Perry, 1993). This impaired stress response can affect physical and mental health throughout life (Cooke, 2008; Perry, 1993).

We cannot eliminate all stress for children. Even if we could, it would not be desirable to do so. Some stress is a part of normal development. For example, learning to walk, toilet training and starting school are stressors. As adults, we need to minimize chronic stressors for children and teach them skills to deal with common everyday stressors.

Some stressors that we can and should minimize include large class sizes, negative relationships and unrealistic adult expectations. Children need positive environments at home, child care and school. Children need and deserve to be treated with respect. This will help them learn respect for others.

Clues to a child's stress triggers can be evident in children's behavior, play, sleep and eating patterns. Observation and communication are helpful in identifying stressors.

Teach Children to Handle Stress

1. Help children view situations as a challenge. Occasionally provide new activities. When new activities are commonplace, children learn they can cope with new situations.

2. Acknowledge children's feelings and be considerate. Comments such as, "I understand you are upset about…" validate children's feelings. Teach children to use feeling words, such as happy and sad.

3. Teach life skills. Give children tasks which they are capable of handling. Make sure they complete the tasks and offer praise. This improves self-esteem and teaches children they are competent to handle daily life and its stress.

4. Help children learn coping techniques. Exercise and eating a balanced diet help elevate mood. Unstructured play, hobbies, art, music and drama can help children cope with stress and make sense of their world.

5. Be a good role model.

Child Wise Learning

Environments for Calm Behaviors
- Furniture Arrangement
- Traffic Paths
- Colors
- Sounds
- Lighting
- Fragrances
- Private Areas
- Slow Rocking Activities

CHAPTER 5

How to Design Calm Physical Environments

Imagine walking into a dinner party where the table is formally set with soft lighting and soft music. Would this environment affect your behavior? Would your behavior be different if the table was set with paper plates? What if the table setting was red and the music was rock?

Environmental design techniques, including careful use of color, are used by businesses to market their products. Formal restaurants use soft music and dim lights to create a romantic setting, letting carpets absorb sounds. Informal restaurants have louder music and hard floors, to create a more casual environment. Department stores play soft music to encourage shoppers to relax, stay longer, and spend more money.

Creating a Safe Haven for Children

Children, like adults, respond to their environments – either positively or negatively. Space design plays a key role in children's interaction with toys, other children and adults.

Creating calm environments can help prevent behavior problems, decrease stress, and teach children how to self-calm. When environments are less stressful, behavior and learning improve. Furniture arrangement, traffic paths, colors, sounds, lighting and fragrances play a role in creating calm environments.

Furniture Arrangement and Traffic Paths

When arranging furniture, consider traffic paths and your own goals. If your goal is for children to run or ride toys, arrange open spaces that will accommodate this. On the other hand, if your goal is to decrease active play in a certain area, arrange furniture to block potential running spaces.

Having well-defined areas helps children know where things belong. For example, when the block area is defined, a child has a better understanding of where the blocks belong. Areas can be defined by furniture arrangement, area rugs, curtains or other devices. Quiet areas should be separate from loud areas.

Colors

The effect of colors on mood varies with individuals and cultures. Some cultures associate black with mourning, while others consider white as the color for grief. Bold colors energize some people, while over-stimulating others. Although the psychology of color varies with individuals, there are some general considerations when designing spaces.

Red – stimulates and energizes.

> In children's spaces, this color would be better used as an accent, such as toys or a pillow, rather than an entire room. Too much of this color could be over-stimulating for infants and hyperactive children.

Green – symbolizes the balance in nature.

> Adding green plants to a room helps create balance and harmony.

Blue – conveys peace and tranquility.

> This color is considered non-threatening.

When used appropriately, colors can change the appearance of a room. Dark colors make large rooms appear smaller. Tall ceilings will appear shorter when painted a shade darker than the walls. Light colors make small rooms appear larger and low ceilings appear higher.

Lighting

Light affects productivity and mood. Some research indicates that natural light improves learning and mood while decreasing days missed from school (Jensen, 1998). When room design prohibits the use of natural light, full-spectrum lights can be used.

Sounds

Many children, and adults, are sensitive to high noise levels.

Some children, especially those with a sensitive nervous system, may become over-stimulated when exposed to excessive noise. They may be more prone to cry or become hyperactive. Children who have been abused or have experienced other types of trauma may become withdrawn or aggressive when adults yell.

Attention to the type and level of sounds can be a tool in improving behavior and learning.

• Soft, slow music decreases stress and heart rate. Children who have experienced trauma need music that is about 80 beats per minute (Perry, 2008).

• Carpeting or rugs on floors and/or walls helps absorb noise.

• Adults who use soft, calm voices promote a safe environment.

Fragrances

While more research is needed in this area, some studies indicate that fragrances do affect the brain. Most of us prefer the smell of potpourri to dirty diapers. Fragrances come in many forms including oils, sprays and natural forms, such as oranges or fresh-baked bread. Hot oil fragrances and some plants are not recommended around young children because of potential safety hazards. **Before using any type of fragrance, always consider children's safety and allergies.**

Private Areas

Every child needs a private space where he or she can occasionally be alone. This could be the child's room, a bean bag or pillow in the corner, a space under a table or a small loft built for this purpose. Equip this area with items that promote self-calm, such as books, puzzles, or soft music.

Rocking

The slow motion of rocking calms the nervous system (Perry, 2008). This is helpful for all children, but it is especially helpful for children who have experienced trauma or those with sensory integration issues. Rocking chairs, balancing balls and swings can be used for the rocking motion that children need. Motion can be incorporated with various areas. For example, a child's rocking chair can be included in a private area while swings and balls can be included in active areas.

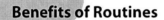

Benefits of Routines
- Provide a predictable environment
- Decrease stress
- Improve relationships
- Improve learning

CHAPTER 6

The Essentials of Predictable Routines

The toddler was accustomed to arriving at child care each morning at 7:30 a.m. The routine was consistent. They had morning activities and snacks, lunch, and naps. After naps, they had snacks and free play. His mother consistently returned for him at 4 p.m. each day. Every day, he went to the door to watch for her about five or ten minutes before she arrived. The family child care provider thought he judged the time by the departure of other children. One day, the other children were not there. The toddler still waited by the door for his mother at 4 p.m. He knew the routine.

Children need a predictable environment. Routines provide that predictability. Children who have regular daily routines are healthier and have better self-regulation of behavior. Predictable routines decrease stress, improve family relationships and improve academic achievement

(Fiese, 2002). Common family routines include mealtimes, household chores, bedtime and regular daily activities. Daily routines for young children may also include snack time and nap time. Unlike strict schedules, routines may have some flexibility in time, but the time should not vary greatly.

Transitions

Moving from one activity or place to another can be difficult for young children. When adults expect children to instantly stop one activity and refocus on another one, the result may be a temper tantrum. The stress of changing activities can be decreased by using a transitional activity. Giving a five-to-ten minute warning will let children know that it is almost time to change activities. Sometimes, another activity will be need for a smooth transition. For example, before naptime, give children a warning that it is almost time to pick up toys and prepare for naps. At the end of the warning time, help children pick up toys. Then read a story together. After the story, let each child choose books to "read" while resting.

Transitions between home and child care or school can be especially difficult for young children, as well as teachers and parents. Consistent daily routines help children know what to expect. Rituals, such as using a timer to help dawdling preschoolers stay on task when getting dressed, help children adapt to hurried morning schedules. Teachers can use various morning greeting exercises to ease the transition. Some teachers use classroom charts or stickers for children to express their feeling while starting the day. Helping individual children plan their day is another way to transition. At the end of the day, teachers can review activities for the day and remind children to tell their parents what they did. Parents can ease the transition by taking a few minutes to hold and play with children before starting household tasks. This will calm children, whose day may have been as stressful as their parents.

Meals and Snacks

Young children need frequent meals and snacks. Irregular eating is typical for young children. Providing healthy snacks mid-morning, mid-afternoon and evening can balance poor eating at mealtimes. Routine times for meals and snacks should be established. More information on feeding young children is included in Chapter 7.

Activities

Daily routines should provide a mix of activities. Alternating active and quiet times helps prevent behavior problems caused by over-stimulation. Play should include time for group play and time to play alone. Both are important for learning self-regulation. Likewise, both active and quiet play are needed to develop skills.

Chores

Chores, both at home and at preschool, can be part of the daily routine. With adult assistance and supervision, young children can participate in doing simple chores that are safe and age-appropriate. Children can easily become frustrated when tasks are too difficult for them. Pairing younger children with an older child or adult can help alleviate this problem. A two-year-old could help pick up toys, set the table or toss a salad, but most two-year-olds could not and would not perform these tasks alone. Preschool and elementary school-aged children can help with simple food preparation, clearing the table and taking care of pets. Including children in simple, age-appropriate chores helps build self-esteem and self-regulation.

Sleep

Many children are sleep deprived. They resist naps and nighttime sleep. They have difficulty going to sleep at night and staying asleep. This can be a result of consuming caffeine, watching TV in the bedroom or a simple lack of

Sample Daily Routine

Approximate Time	Activity
7:30 – 8:00 a.m.	Breakfast
8:00 – 9:30 a.m.	Quiet play with books, puzzles, building materials, art project, etc.
9:30-10:00 a.m.	Mid-morning snack
10:00-11:30 a.m.	Active play with riding toys, swings, balls, pretend play, etc.
11:30-12:00 a.m.	Transition for lunch by picking up toys, washing hands, and helping set table
12:00-12:30	Lunch
12:30- 1:00 p.m.	Transition for naps/rest by cleaning table and reading a story
1:00- 3:00 p.m.	Nap or rest time and quiet play for non- sleepers
3:00 – 3:30 p.m.	Mid-afternoon snack
3:30 – 5:30 p.m.	Active play
5:30 – 6:00 p.m.	Transition for dinner by helping prepare dinner or quiet play
6:00 – 6:45 p.m.	Dinner
6:45 – 7:30 p.m.	Transition for bedtime routine by cleaning table and taking baths
7-30 – 8:30 p.m.	Bedtime routine – snacks, books, games
8:30 p.m.	Bedtime

Child Wise Learning

routine and parental expectations (National Sleep Foundation, 2004). The lack of sleep then results in hyperactivity and cranky behaviors. Indeed, researchers have linked sleep deprivation to attention deficit/hyperactivity disorder (ADHD) (National Sleep Foundation, 2002). Children who are sleep deprived are at an increased risk of injury, obesity and respiratory problems (National Sleep Foundation, 2001). Lack of sleep decreases alertness and attention. It also has a negative affect on emotions, thought processes and motor activity (National Sleep Foundation, 2006).

Bedtime struggles and nighttime waking can be decreased by regular bedtime routines. The routine should include 20 to 30 minutes of quiet time before naps and bedtime. This could include a bath, story, puzzles, quiet games or soft music. It is not the time for television, computers, active play or exercise.

Foods that children eat, or don't eat, are directly related to health, brain function, and stress management.

CHAPTER 7

Nutrition: Fuel for Body, Learning, and Behavior

The young girl looked at the vegetable garden with amazement. She asked what the green beans were. These beans looked different from green beans out of a can. She wanted to know why the tomatoes were changing from a green color to yellow and red. She wasn't sure she wanted to eat tomatoes that grew in the dirt. When she later learned that milk comes from dairy cows, she said, "I like milk from the store."

The preschoolers looked at the homemade macaroni and cheese. Typically, macaroni and cheese was one of their favorite foods, but the homemade version didn't look like the macaroni and cheese made from the box. The macaroni was larger and it wasn't bright yellow. They refused to eat this unfamiliar food.

Few of today's children have the experience of learning the origin of their foods. They have less exposure to the taste and smell of fresh foods that are grown in backyard gardens and prepared in family kitchens than previous generations. With more meals eaten outside the home or prepared from convenience foods, children have developed a taste for processed foods with artificial ingredients.

Children's food choices are also influenced by advertising. Companies target their marketing to children through television commercials and branding of their products. Company branding of products has a stronger influence on children's food preferences than taste and smell (Robinson, Borzekowski, Matheson, & Kraemer, 2007). Children notice these brands on signs and products. The products are typically placed at a child's eye level on store shelves.

Nutrition and Health

Malnutrition means bad nutrition. Malnutrition can be the result of poor food choices or inadequate food consumption. In third-world countries, malnourished children typically display symptoms of extreme underweight or distended stomachs, which is a sign of protein deficiency. Symptoms of malnourished children in more affluent nations may be more subtle and displayed as overweight. Children can have their stomachs full and still be malnourished. Eating foods that fill the stomach, but do not provide the nutrients that the body needs to function properly can result in malnutrition.

The rapid increase of childhood obesity in America has been well publicized in recent years. While overweight or obesity can be a result of poor food choices, it can also be a result of children living in poverty. Children who live in low-income families have a higher risk of becoming overweight or obese (Hass, et al., 2003; Johnson & Theberge, 2007).

Children who are overweight have an increased risk of diabetes, joint problems, high blood pressure, asthma, low self-esteem and school performance (Waring, & Lapane, 2008; CDC, 2008).

Symptoms of Short-Term Hunger
• Reading and Math Difficulty
• Decreased Attention Span
• Difficulty Interacting with Environment
• Irritability and Frustration
• Behavior Problems
• Decreased Energy
• Headache
• Trembling
• Nausea
• Apathy

Child Wise
Learning

Food choices affect children's health issues, learning and behavior. Some diseases begin in childhood and have been linked to diet and lifestyle. This includes clogged arteries and high blood pressure, which lead to heart disease. Eating a balanced diet plays in a role in disease prevention, stress management, concentration and memory.

Nutrition and Behavior

The connection between diet and behavior has been and remains a controversial issue in this country. For over thirty years, the Feingold Association has advocated a diet free of additives to calm behaviors. While some parents and teachers are convinced that sugar causes hyperactivity, research has not found a connection. The hyperactivity associated with sugar may actually be from other foods that are mixed with the sugar, such as artificial food coloring or preservatives. A recent British study did find a connection between children's hyperactivity and artificial food coloring and preservatives (Doheny, 2007).

Another study from Purdue University found low blood levels of omega-3 fatty acids among boys with behavior problems (Purdue News, 1996). Omega 3 fats are found in fatty fish, flax seed, nuts,canola and olive oils.

Some studies have found a possible connection between hyperactivity and food allergies in a small percentage of children. This does not mean that all hyperactive children have allergies and react to colorings and preservatives, but we should be aware that anyone can have allergies or sensitivities to any food.

Current research indicates that hunger or food insecurity is a factor in children's behavior. Hunger can increase fatigue, hyperactivity, apathy, irritability and behavior problems (Broberg, Broberg, & McGuire, 2009; Medline Plus, 2008; Pierson 1998).

Therefore, when a child is displaying behavior problems, dietary evaluation should be part of the observation process in determining possible causes for the behavior. Recording a child's behavior before and after eating can be effective in identifying foods that trigger behavior problems. A registered dietician or nutritionist can provide additional assistance, if needed.

Nutrition and Learning

The relationship between nutrition and learning is well established (Medline Plus, 2008; Pierson, 1998). Poor nutrition has a negative effect on learning. Short-term hunger, such as a missed breakfast, can decrease attention, energy, reading and math abilities (Pierson, 1998).

Just as the teeth, skin, heart and other body organs need nutrients, the brain also needs nutrients to function optimally. There is no one food that will meet all the needs of the brain. All nutrients – vitamins, minerals, carbohydrates, protein, fat and water – play a role. A variety of foods is necessary to supply all the needed nutrients.

Vitamins are needed to develop and protect neurotransmitters, chemicals that help the brain cells communicate (Somer, 1996). Several of the B vitamins and vitamin C are needed for short-term memory and problem solving. Folic acid (a B vitamin) and vitamin B12 assist the blood cells that carry oxygen to the brain. Good sources for these nutrients include cereals, pastas, breads, eggs, milk, dark-green leafy vegetables, and fruits.

Minerals play a role in optimal brain function. Mild iron deficiency can decrease attention, concentration, and memory while increasing irritability and fatigue. Good sources of iron are meats, beans, whole-grains, dark-green vegetables, eggs, shrimp and oysters. Other minerals that support brain function include copper, iodine, zinc, sodium, potassium, chloride, calcium and magnesium. These are found in whole grains, nuts, legumes, meats, milk and some fruits and vegetables.

Carbohydrates and proteins are also necessary for the brain's neurotransmitters. Complex carbohydrates, such as pasta and bread, increase energy and productivity. Sugar is a simple carbohydrate and will produce energy for a short period of time after which there is a sharp decline in energy. This is known as the mid-morning slump, a rapid decline in energy. Eating complex carbohydrates, found in whole-grain breads and cereals, will produce energy for a longer time period. Carbohydrates promote relaxation. Protein, on the other hand, increases alertness. Meals containing carbohydrates and proteins increase both energy and alertness. Protein is found in meat, milk, fish, legumes, vegetables, grains and nuts.

Symtpoms of Prolonged Hunger
- Decreased Immunity
- Difficulty Concentrating
- Social-Emotional Misbehavior
- Growth Impairment
- Fatigue
- Irritability
- Dizziness

Child Wise Learning

Fat is needed for brain growth and development in young children. Mother's milk and infant formulas contain the fat needed for rapid brain growth during the infant and young toddler stages. After the second birthday, fat can be decreased, but should not be eliminated completely. Some fat is necessary for the absorption of vitamins A, D, E and K. Fatty fish, nuts, flax seed, canola and olive oils provide healthy omega 3 fatty acids which support the fat soluble vitamins and brain function.

Water helps dissolve nutrients and carry them throughout the body, including the brain. Mild dehydration can negatively affect energy, attention and memory (Jensen, 1998; Hannaford, 2005). Children should be encouraged to drink water throughout the day.

Self-regulation of Eating

Children generally have inconsistent eating patterns. This is normal and usually is not a cause for concern. Their food intake will probably be adequate over an extended period of time. It is never appropriate to force children to eat. Doing so can increase the risk of obesity and eating disorders. Learning to eat in a healthy manner is a process that is part of self-regulation. Here are some suggestions for helping children develop good eating habits.

• Involve children in gardening, meal planning and food preparation. Children are more likely to eat what they have helped prepare. Preschool children can help place food in the grocery cart, toss a salad or set the table. Elementary-aged children can begin learning how to read food labels and recipes.

- Serve breakfast daily, even if it is not always eaten. Studies indicate that children who eat breakfast are better learners (Medline Plus, 2008). Be sure to include bread, fruit or fruit juice and a meat or meat alternate, such as eggs or milk. Remember that breakfast doesn't have to consist of eggs or cereal. Some children prefer non-traditional breakfast foods.

- Provide mid-morning and mid-afternoon snacks. Serving healthy snacks will help balance poorly eaten meals.

- When planning meals, include a variety of colors and textures. Finger foods are always favorites.

- Introduce no more than one new food at a time and serve it with a favorite food. Plan to offer the new food ten to fifteen times before deciding the food is not liked. Time is needed to learn to like some foods.

- Encourage a healthy attitude toward food. Moderation and variety are the keys to healthy eating. Candy and ice cream are acceptable in moderation. These can be limited by the amount that is purchased.

- De-emphasize desserts. Desserts should not be treated as special foods. Dessert can be fruit served with the main course.

Child Food intake

Date	Time	Food/drink consumed	Where consumed	Feelings before	Feelings after

Aspects of Communication
Verbal
- What we say
- How we say it
- Tone of voice

Non-verbal
- Posture
- Gestures
- Facial Expressions

Listening
- Stop and pay attention
- Make eye-contact
- "Hear" what is being said

CHAPTER 8

How to Communicate
Needs and Feelings

The grandmother gave the nine-month-old a cracker. Then she proceeded to get a different kind of cracker for herself. He sat in the high chair, holding his cracker in front of his face. He looked back and forth from his cracker to grandmother's cracker and then back to his. Noticing his body language, the grandmother gave him a cracker just like hers, while talking to him about the crackers. At fifteen months of age, this child used sign language to sign "cracker" when he wanted one. As his verbal skills improved, his sign language gradually decreased.

Communication involves more than speaking words. It includes nonverbal communication, listening and responding.

Nonverbal communication includes body language, such as raising the eyebrows, making eye contact, or looking away. Listening includes paying attention while a person is talking and responding. Responses can be clarified by paraphrasing what you think you heard. Rewording the message and sending it back gives an opportunity to clarify any misunderstanding.

Effective communication respects the thoughts and feelings of others. It includes open-ended questions and "I" messages. Using open-ended questions that start with could, would or how are more likely to generate a response. Questions that can be answered with "yes" or "no" are not likely to generate a discussion. "I" messages convey trust and respect while "you" messages indicate blame. Saying, "I feel…" opens communication.

Young children need to learn how to express their feelings and needs. This is a process that requires physical maturation of muscles, thinking processes and modeling by adults. Just as the muscles in the legs need to support walking, the muscles around the mouth must be developed to support verbal communication. Simple sign language is effective in helping young children communicate basic needs before they gain the physical ability to verbalize their needs. Gradually the muscles and vocabulary will increase, but these alone will not be sufficient without adults taking time to help children learn how to communicate. The foundation for communication skills occurs in early childhood. Communication skills learned in the early years have lifelong effects. If effective communication skills are not learned in childhood, adult relationships will be negatively affected (Weinhold & Weinhold, 2008a; Weinhold & Weinhold, 2008b).

Learning to communicate effectively takes time, practice and patience. When communicating with children, get down on their level and look at their eyes while you talk. Keep your voice firm and relaxed. There is no need to yell. Children will be more likely to pay attention if you speak in a normal tone of voice.

Teachable moments in daily living are perfect times to model and teach effective communication. Talk about feelings, such as happy, sad, glad, hungry and tired.

Communication skills also play a role in conflict resolution. This simple model can be used as a tool for addressing conflict.

1. Describe the situation.

("When the toys are not picked up before lunch....")

2. Tell how the child's behavior interferes with your life, using "I" messages.

("I have to pick them up by myself while you are napping.")

3. Express your feelings with "I" messages.

("...and I don't like having to pick them up by myself.")

4. State what you want the child to do.

("I would like you to help me pick up the toys before lunch. Will you help me?")

5. State consequences only if you are willing to carry out the consequence. ("If I have to pick up the toys by myself, I will put them high in the closet where no one can play with them for the rest of the day.")

PART 3

Emotions and Behavior

Emotions, learning and behavior are all interconnected.

A torn jacket is soon mended; but
hard words bruise the heart of a child.

—H.W. LONGFELLOW

The *Process* of Learning Self-Regulation

Infants
- Do not have the physical ability to self-calm
- Calmed by rocking, soft music, gentle touch and familiar voices
- Emotionally connect with primary caregiver through eye contact
- Imitate vocal sounds and facial expressions
- Attach to primary caregiver

Toddlers
- Use self-talk to help regulate behavior
- Developing an awareness for other people's feelings, the beginning of empathy
- Calmed by transitional objects, such as blankets and special toys
- Learning independence skills, such as self-feeding, dressing and toileting
- Learning to separate from primary caregiver

Preschoolers
- Make simple choices related to eating, dressing, toileting and playing
- Increased ability to verbally express needs and emotions
- Learn peer approval and disapproval through play
- Learn negotiation skills through play

Primary school-aged children
- More logic thinking skills due to jump in cognitive development
- Likes orderly rules and fairness for everything
- Developing skills for delayed gratification

CHAPTER 9

Emotions:
Learning to Self-Regulate

The kindergartener was consistently disruptive in the classroom. His inability to regulate his behavior was interfering with learning for the entire class. The teacher frequently left him in time-out so she could teach the other children.

This scenario is repeated in numerous classrooms every year. Preschool and kindergarten teachers are reporting increasing numbers of young children with behavior problems (National Scientific Council on the Developing Child, 2008).

Emotional development is more critical than intellectual development in learning (Goleman, 1995; National Scientific Council on the Developing Child, 2008). Children who have difficulty regulating their behavior will have difficulty regulating learning and life skills.

Emotional development is the development of social skills, sometimes called social competence. These skills include understanding feelings, learning to read facial expressions, having empathy for others, learning to manage personal emotions and regulate behaviors (National Scientific Council on the Developing Child, 2004).

The Process of Learning Self-Regulation

Learning to calm and self-regulate behavior is a *process* that begins in infancy and continues throughout childhood and adolescence. Newborns do not have the ability to self-regulate their emotions and behavior. This skill will gradually be developed throughout childhood. This process is interconnected with the development of the nervous system, communication skills, thinking processes and adult-child interactions (McDevitt & Ormrod, 2002; National Scientific Council on the Developing Child, 2004; Weinhold & Weinhold, 2007).

Infants have little ability to regulate their emotions. They biologically cannot do this because their nervous systems are immature. As they interact with caregivers, especially their mothers, they learn to make eye contact and imitate facial expressions. This interaction and sensory exchange gradually forms an adult-child attachment and emotional connections in the brain. This is the foundation for emotional development. Gentle, positive touch is especially important for the baby to connect with the adult. Without adequate touch, the infant may not form an emotional attachment to the primary caregiver and could fail to thrive in development (Weinhold & Weinhold, 2007).

Toddlers have gained enough maturation of the nervous system to walk, run and begin to talk. They may use self-talk as a tool to explain actions. "Me do it" is a common phrase for this stage. They are becoming more aware of feelings and emotions. It is not unusual for one toddler to cry in response to another child's cries. This is a sign that the toddler is developing an awareness of other people's feelings, the beginning of empathy.

Preschoolers gradually refine their understanding of feelings and emotions. Increased vocabulary makes it easier to communicate their emotions, but they may still need help doing so. As they interact with peers through play, they develop skills for self-regulation and interacting with others.

Primary school-aged children have a better understanding of other people's thoughts and feelings. They are now fluent with their primary language and have better reasoning skills. This makes it easier for them to use words to express feelings and emotions. Rules are popular at this stage. If a game doesn't have rules, the children will invent some. This is an indication that they are learning to comply with societal rules and self-regulate their behaviors (McDevitt & Ormrod, 2002).

Emotions and Learning

As children interact with their environments, they experience emotions. These emotions then form connections in their brains. The neural circuits formed from emotions interact with the circuits that are used for thinking skills, such as planning and decision-making (National Scientific

Council on the Developing Child, 2004). This is why it is easier to remember something that involves emotion. Emotions, learning and behavior are inter-connected.

Regulating emotions is essential for optimal learning. Controlled emotions support learning, while unregulated emotions interfere with thinking and learning processes (National Scientific Council on the Developing Child, 2004). Children who develop a good emotional foundation before they begin kindergarten will be more successful in formal education, lifelong learning and lifelong relationships.

Emotions and Life Skills

The emotional development of the early years forms the foundation for life's relationships. This includes skills needed for future employment and parenting (National Scientific Council on the Developing Child, 2004). Environments that deprive young children of positive sensory and socio-emotional stimulation

---

Teaching Self-Regulation
Model and teach positive relationships
- Use positive touch
- Talk about feelings, such as happy, sad, tired and hungry
- Play games making and guessing facial expressions

Teach stress coping skills (See chapter on stress)
- Create a private space with calming activities
- Maintain a balanced life style

Encourage independence and decision-making skills
- Allow children to make age-appropriate decisions
- Include children in planning and choosing activities
- Involve children in simple household chores
- Encourage self-help skills
- Teach simple conflict and decision-making skills, such as "Let's find something for you to do while you wait for your turn with the toy."

Child Wise Learning

can impair the formation of brain circuits, compromising future development (National Scientific Council on the Developing Child, 2007). A poor emotional foundation in the early years increases the possibility of high risk behaviors in adulthood, such as addictions (Weinhold & Weinhold, 2007).

Relationships are essential in early emotional development. Supportive relationships can buffer difficult environments while the harmful effects of non-supportive relationships can extend into adulthood (National Scientific Council on the Developing Child, 2008). Adult-child relationships, especially during the infant and toddler stages of development, will be replayed in relationships throughout life (Weinhold & Weinhold, 2007). Supportive adults are essential for modeling and teaching age-appropriate self-regulation skills.

Common Age-Related Behaviors*

The Young Infant
- Cries to express needs and emotions

The Older Infant
- Puts everything into mouth
- Bangs cup with a spoon
- Likes to put fingers in mouth

The One-Year Old
- Enjoys throwing things, including food
- Gets into everything
- May refuse to cooperate with daily routines
- Plays alone
- Likes to chase and be chased
- Appetite decreases as growth slows
- Likes to climb
- Dislikes going to bed

The Two-Year-Old
- "Do It Myself" stage
- Possessive of toys
- Curious
- Difficulty making choices
- Behavior extremes

The Three-Year-Old
- More open to suggestions
- Can make simple choices
- Likes to talk, including tattling
- Tells others what to do
- May have an imaginary playmate
- Defends possessions, often aggressively
- Nightmares and fears are common
- Sharing and taking turns are difficult

The Four-Year-Old
- Full of questions
- Talkative
- Appears self-centered
- Boastful and bossy
- Mood changes rapidly
- Calls others names
- Plays with a group of friends

The Five-Year-Old
- Emotions are more stable
- Likes to be independent
- Likes to be a helper
- Hits and pushes classmates
- Prefers playing with one or two special friends

The Six-Year-Old
- Free with opinions
- Tends to be a know-it-all
- Easier to observe rules
- Likes games with rules

The Seven-Year-Old
- Complains of unfair treatment
- Wants to be one of the gang
- Impatient

The Eight-Year-Old
- Peer group is important
- Reacts to groups approval
- Accepts some responsibility for actions

*These behaviors are related to ages and stages of development. See Part 1 of this book.

CHAPTER 10

Common Behaviors:
Prevention and Response

A child hits, kicks, bites and has tantrums. Another child withdraws into his inner self, having little interaction with others. Should adults be concerned about these behaviors? What can be done when time-out doesn't work?

Children are not born knowing how to behave. They learn as they grow, develop and interact with other people and their environments. They are in the *process* of learning social skills. Therefore, behaviors will vary according to the child's age, health, environment, personal relationships and stress response.

As adults, it is our responsibility to nurture and teach our children. Our expectations need to be realistic according to the child's age. When children feel safe and understood, negative behaviors will usually decrease.

Why Children Misbehave

Children's behavior is typically a developmental response to events in the environment. Misbehavior is often triggered by new or stressful events, such as moving or getting a new sibling. Young children who are hungry, thirsty, or sleepy are more inclined to misbehave. Some behaviors are for the purpose of seeking attention. If positive adult attention is lacking, problematic behaviors may become a routine manner of seeking attention. Children tend to repeat behavior that gets them attention. From a child's perspective, negative attention is better than no attention.

The Role of Temperament

Temperament plays a role in individual children's responses to the environment (National Scientific Council on the Developing Child, 2008). A child who is sensitive may cry more easily. An easy-going child may have a high tolerance for stress, while a child with a more aggressive personality may have a lower tolerance. Understanding and predicting a child's behavioral response is critical in preventing and dealing with behavior issues.

Preventing Misbehavior

Childhood behaviors are intertwined with adult expectations and interactions. This interconnection of behavior with the environment provides an opportunity to prevent and manage behaviors by adjusting the environment. Children have an internal need for things that are familiar. Negative behaviors can be decreased by adding some structure and clarifying adult expectations.

Have predictable routines. Daily routines and schedules provide familiar environments while helping regulate hunger, thirst, sleep and stress.

Have a few rules. Clear and consistent rules help children know what is expected of them. The rules must be short and age-appropriate. Young children cannot remember a long list of rules. Simple rules can be developed in family and classroom meetings.

Teach communication and decision-making skills. Teaching children how to make simple choices, resolve problems, express needs and describe feelings are tools for regulating behavior.

Provide private spaces for self-calming. Providing a quiet, safe, non-threatening place where a child can retreat is often an effective tool to help learn self-calming techniques. Include calming activities in this area, such as books and soft music. A child who *begins* to lose control should be directed to the private area for time to self-calm.

Give attention to positive behavior. Compliment children who are playing nicely. This lets children know they can get adult attention without misbehaving.

Use family and classroom meetings to involve children in simple group decisions. These can be brief and informal. Group meetings can be used to plan activities, address issues or develop rules.

Identifying Behavior Triggers

Triggers for misbehavior can often be identified by observing a child's behavior in the context of the surrounding environment of home, child care,

Techniques for Behavior Intervention

Following are some methods of dealing with young children's behavior. A child's stage of development and personal needs should always be considered when choosing a method of behavior intervention.

Redirection – The child is directed to an appropriate activity. For example, when a child throws a large truck, the truck is replaced with a soft ball that can be thrown. This method works well for toddlers.

Positive Reinforcement – The adult lets the child know what behavior is acceptable by showing approval of good behavior. Hugs, smiles, eye contact, and verbal communication can convey behavioral acceptance.

Ignoring Unacceptable Behaviors – This method can be used with positive reinforcement, but should be used minimally and only if the child is not hurting someone. This is often effective for temper tantrums at home or in the classroom.

Private time – The child is moved to a private place for self-calming.

Natural and Logical Consequences – Discipline is related to the behavior. For example, a child who colors on the wall, gets to help clean the it.

Problem-Solving – This simple form of conflict resolution works well with preschool and elementary-aged children. Adults guide children in choosing possible solutions. The pros and cons are discussed. A solution is selected and implemented. If the solution doesn't work, the situation is re-evaluated.

Family/Classroom Meetings – Group meetings can be used to plan events, develop rules or address issues. The meetings can be informal or formal. Short, informal meetings are best for preschoolers. School-aged children can gradually be introduced to a more formal structure with a meeting agenda and minutes.

Child Wise
Learning

school and community. It is important to be objective and keep a written record. The written report does not include the adult's interpretation of the event. For example, if Susie hits Johnnie while they are playing with blocks, the observation record would be "Susie hit Johnnie while they were playing with blocks." A record, such as, "I think Susie hit Johnnie because…." would be biased because it includes the adult's opinion, which may not be correct. Observation records, kept over a period of time, may show a pattern of behaviors related to certain times, people, or events. Once the behavior triggers are identified, steps can be taken to address the issues that are triggering the misbehavior. A sample observation form is included in this section. Completed forms should be filed and used for future reference. When completing the form, consider the following issues:

Evaluate the misbehavior scene.

Who is present when the behavior occurs?

What activity is occurring? Record the specific activity, such as playing with blocks, mealtime, or shopping.

When does the behavior problem occur? Does it consistently occur around mealtime or bedtime? If the issue is related to mealtimes, perhaps the child is hungry or having an adverse food reaction. If it is related to bedtime, perhaps making a change in the bedtime routine would help. Is the behavior related to playtime? If so, is it associated with a certain activity?

Where does the behavior problem occur? Is it in the child's home, child care, school, or another public place?

Notice possible signs of stress. Pay attention to shallow breathing, cold hands and rapid heartbeat.

Evaluate the child's dietary habits. What has the child had to eat that day? Is there a pattern of behavior problems when meals are missed? Is there a pattern of behavior problems associated with certain foods?

Consider motor, neurological, sensory and social skills. Are there signs of developmental delays? If so, the behavior may be related to these. Pay special attention to these during play. Children who are not good players may be lacking in these areas.

Careful observation can help identify behavior triggers. Then a plan can be formed to deal with the behavior. Sometimes, the solution can be as simple as making a change in the environment or daily routine. For example, a child who consistently misbehaves at lunchtime may need an earlier lunch. Professional intervention may be needed for some behaviors. This will be covered in Chapter 11.

The Attuned Teacher

The new preschool teacher had invited me to see what she had done with the classroom. She introduced herself and showed me the classroom. Using paper-mache, she had transformed the classroom into a picture of an island oasis. There were paper-mache trees all over the classroom. The green color gave a sense of calm.

One child in this classroom had exhibited some difficult behaviors with previous teachers. He had urinated in the corner. With one swipe of the hand, he could throw all the toys off the shelves. I observed his behavior with this new teacher. When it was music time, the teacher reminded him that he was her helper. It was his job to turn on the music and keep it playing. When it was time for outside play, she again reminded him that he was her helper. Did he remember the water and drinking cups? The teacher was attuned to the needs of this child. He was helping her, as he grinned from ear to ear. The new teacher had transformed the classroom and the life of a child.

Child Wise Learning

Child Behavior Observation

Date	Time	Food/drink	Activity	Persons present	Behavior symptoms

Behaviors that Need Further Evaluation

• Long, frequent, hard crying that cannot be calmed.

• Child does not wrap arms and legs around the adult when picked up, but hangs like a rag doll.

• Difficulty making and maintaining eye contact, unless this is the part of the child's culture.

• Child fails to grow and develop properly.

• Significant delays in any area of development.

• Child is abusive to animals and/or people.

• Child appears withdrawn and disconnected.

• Child does not engage in play that uses the imagination. Play is either non-existent or only imitates scenes seen on TV or in the movies.

• Child does not want to participate when activities require use of underdeveloped senses.

CHAPTER 11

Behaviors that Require Special Attention

As I entered the chaotic preschool classroom, two boys ran over to see who I was. One asked, "What are you doing here?"' Obviously, they were checking to make sure I would not harm them. As I expected, they were the ones the teacher wanted me to observe. I quickly noticed that the other children were staying away from the boys.

The Importance of Intervention

Some children have difficulty regulating behavior due to certain health problems or traumatic events that have occurred in their lives. Others simply display difficult behaviors because they have additional needs that are not being met. These children need the same basic environments that other children need. However, they may require additional intervention.

Trauma can result from a number of issues, ranging from unmet psychological needs during serious illness and tragic life events to child abuse and neglect. Left untreated, trauma can interfere with early brain development. On a long-term basis, it can negatively impact mental and physical health for life (National Scientific Council on the Developing Child, 2008; Perry, 2008; Weinhold & Weinhold, 2008a; Weinhold & Weinhold, 2008b).

While professional intervention is essential to preventing lifelong problems, finding needed resources can be a major challenge. Few mental health professionals are trained to work with young children. In addition, mental health problems are more difficult to identify in young children (National Scientific Council on the Developing Child, 2008). Finding help for physical health problems can be just as difficult. Busy professionals may not notice subtle signs of problems, such as developmental delays, food allergies or sensory integration difficulties. Gifted children are often unidentified and considered difficult, rather than children who need support services.

More research clearly needs to be done on how to identify and treat problems in young children. Intervention is essential for these children to learn calming behaviors. If help is not received, parents and teachers may have difficulty forming attachments with them. This dramatically increases the potential lifelong problems of these children.

Following are some case histories that offer some insight to identification and intervention. Names and places have been omitted to preserve privacy.

Abuse or Neglect

> *The preschooler took the teacher by the hand and led her into the bathroom. Then he pulled up his pants and said, "Mama hurt me." The teacher noticed scabs in the form of perfect circles all over his body. These were later determined to be cigarette burns.*

As bad as this situation was, there are other cases that are not as easily detected, which can have more devastating lifelong effects. Research indicates that neglect is more difficult for children to overcome than physical or sexual abuse (Blum, 1999).

Physical abuse leaves marks on the body that can be seen. The marks often look like the hand or object that injured the child. As a general rule, these marks are not in places where children typically get scrapes and bruises (Helfer & Kempe, 1987). A physician can usually determine whether the injury was accidental or intentional.

Neglect, on the other hand, is not always easy to detect. Extreme cases that involve lack of physical care, such as bathing or eating, may be detected. However, the more subtle cases that are common in today's society may not be detected. The practice of confining young children in car seats, playpens or baby swings for long periods of time is a form of neglect. Children who spend long hours in front of the television are also neglected. These children, through no fault of their own, are being sentenced to a lifetime of underdeveloped brains. Brain connections are formed by interacting with adults and exploring the environment. Children who are not moving their bodies and their eyes are not forming brain connections (Carnegie Corporation of NY, 1994; Hannaford, 2005).

Sexual and emotional abuse may also be difficult to detect. However, once detected, intervention may be successful in helping these children rebuild their lives.

Common Symptoms

Physical Abuse
 • Marks on the body in the shape of the object that struck the child

Neglect
 • Unclean physical appearance

 • May steal or hoard food

 • May have difficulty concentrating

 • May exhibit withdrawal behaviors, appear out-of-touch

Emotional Abuse
 • Adult is verbally abusive

 • Child may replay abusive behavior while interacting with others

Sexual Abuse
 • May replay abuse behavior through play

 • Possible signs on undergarments

 • May not want to undress around others

Professional Referrals
 • Professionals are required, by law, to report suspected child abuse or neglect. Reports can be made to child protective services or the local police department.

Attachment Disorder

While the mother visited with her friends, the toddler walked around staring at the floor. She did not look up at her mother or her mother's friends. She did not appear concerned about her mother leaving her. When her mother finally picked her up, she hung loose like a rag doll.

The mother called to ask how to deal with her preschooler's behavior. He was throwing the puppies up in the air and catching them.

Both of these children were displaying symptoms of attachment disorder. In both cases, there was an emotional disconnection between mother and child. The toddler was displaying withdrawal by staring at the floor and not interacting with the adults or things in the environment. Remaining limp, instead of putting her arms and legs around the mother are symptoms of attachment disorder. The preschooler's abuse of the puppies indicates a lack of empathy. Both children are high-risk unless these behaviors are reversed.

Common Symptoms
- Symptoms can range from mild to severe
- Mild symptoms may be subtle emotional disconnect
- Child may be withdrawn or aggressive
- Child does not hold onto adult when picked up
- More severe symptoms include abusive behaviors toward people and animals

Professional Referrals
Licensed professional counselors, child psychologists or child psychiatrists who have training and expertise in working with attachment disorder

Attention Deficit Hyperactivity Disorder (ADHD)

The teacher met me in the hallway and quickly explained that she had already talked to the child's mother about putting him on medication for his attention deficit. As I observed in the classroom, I noticed the child frequently found excuses to leave his desk. He needed a bathroom break. He needed a drink of water. He needed to sharpen his pencil. He clearly was having difficulty concentrating. He seemed to be functioning in a mental fog, much as I had previously noticed while he played at child care. After further intervention with the family, questions were raised about possible abuse from a non-family member.

This child was clearly having difficulty concentrating in the classroom environment. From the classroom perspective, this was a concentration issue. However, putting together the big picture of home, child care and school painted a different picture.

Attention Deficit Hyperactive Disorder (ADHD) has become a frequent diagnosis in recent years. The disorder is over-diagnosed often based only on the observation of teachers or parents. This diagnosis should be made by a mental health professional, after the child has received a medical evaluation. Recent research has found that children who have been diagnosed with ADHD have normal brains, but delayed brain maturation (National Institute of Mental Health, 2007).

Stimulant prescription medications have been common treatment. After reports of child deaths, the U.S. Food and Drug Administration (FDA) now requires warnings on some drugs, alerting physicians of the dangers. The American Heart Association recommends that children receive a heart evaluation, including an ECG test, before taking stimulant medications (Medical News Today, 2008).

The American Academy of Pediatrics is encouraging parents to use environmental intervention to treat ADHD. Parents who want more information about medications can discuss it with their child's doctor.

Alternative therapies are becoming more common. These include kid's yoga, pediatric chiropractic, music therapy, dietary changes and various dietary supplements. While improving food choices definitely has benefits, parents should be cautious about giving supplements, other than a multi-vitamin to young children.

The benefits of exercise are well established. We now have confirmation that physical activity improves brain function. John Ratey, M.D., a Harvard professor of psychiatry, refers to exercise as the brain's "Miracle-Gro" (Viadero, 2008). Dr. Ratey believes exercise can replace ADHD medication, at least for some children (ADDitude Magazine, 2008).

Common Symptoms
- Difficulty concentrating
- May be hyperactive
- May have difficulty controlling impulsive behaviors

Professional Referrals
- Pediatrician
- Child Psychologist
- Child Psychiatrist

Gifted Children

The parents requested an observation in their son's elementary class-room. They wanted suggestions on how to deal with his misbehavior at school. As I entered the classroom, I noticed the teacher was breathing shallow breaths and talking rapidly, symptoms of high stress. The child I was there to observe sat, squirming in his chair. I did not observe any misbehavior. When I later met with the family, I found out that the child had been denied recess for about six weeks as a form of punishment. The family eventually decided to place their son in another school where he received daily recess and was placed in a gifted program.

The preschool requested intervention for a five-year-old boy. He frequently became aggressive when the teachers ordered him to comply with their demands. One day, he slapped a teacher. The preschool scheduled a meeting with his mother to decide their next step. They had already considered expulsion. This had happened in previous preschools and the child was distraught over the possibility of another expulsion. The preschool viewed him as a hopeless behavior problem. I saw an extremely bright child who refused to tolerate disrespect from teachers.

There has been an increase of children being expelled from early child-hood programs. It has been my experience that a high percentage of expulsions are gifted children. These children get bored easily and are highly sensitive to the way they are treated by adults. They consider themselves equal to adults and absolutely will not tolerated adult disrespect. They don't like to be told "No," unless they also receive an explanation for why they should not do something. It is not usual for gifted children to have uneven development, advanced development in some areas and delays in other areas. Their behaviors may fluctuate from childish to appearing way beyond their years. They may also have other issues. For example, a child can be gifted and also have special needs (Silverman, 2002).

Common Symptoms
- Easily frustrated and bored
- Consider themselves equal to adults
- Require little sleep
- Right-brain learners – need to see big picture
- May lack ability to understand consequences (a left-brain skill)
- May have uneven development

Professional Referrals
- School Counselor
- Child Psychologist

Sensory Processing Disorder

The child had a difficult start in life. The pregnancy and birth had been difficult. At eleven months, his attention span while playing was exceptionally long, but he preferred quiet play. When he walked, his right leg was slightly twisted. At the age of three, his behavior became more problematic. He ran and screamed uncontrollably when in large stores. When he sat next to others, he would lean into them. When asked to join in active play, he would put his hands in his pockets and shake his head no. At the age of four, he was screened for possible developmental delays, but the screeners didn't think the problems were significant. The pediatrician also didn't detect any delays, but did refer him to a child psychologist for a gifted evaluation. The child psychologist determined that he was gifted, but also noticed uneven development and recommended an evaluation with an occupational therapist. The occupational therapist detected sensory processing disorder. After a year of occupational therapy, his motor skills and behavior improved.

Sensory processing disorder can be a hidden condition and can significantly impact a child's development. The disorder is actually a term that is used to describe a variety of neurological problems. Depending on the specific neurological problem, sleeping, eating, playing, learning and self-regulation can be affected. The disorder may be independent or overlap other conditions, such as ADHD, autism and giftedness (Kranowitz, 2005). This may make detection more difficult. In the above case, the child's giftedness was overshadowing his sensory difficulties, making them harder to detect.

Common Symptoms
- Varies according to specific senses involved
- Under or over sensitive to senses, especially touch
- Delay and difficulty with activities involving motor skills
- Difficulty transitioning between activities
- Difficulty focusing eyes for extended concentration
- May have difficulty eating
- Easily over-stimulated
- May have delay in self-help skills, such as dressing and toileting

Professional Referrals
- Occupational Therapist

Non-Productive Play

The five-year-old boy ran from one activity to another. He looked at the toys, but did not play with them.

The four-year-old looked mean and proceeded to move into a fighting position as he said, "I'm going to send you to outer space." The teacher quickly realized this was a reenactment of a television scene and decided to alter his script. She said, "Oh, what will I do? Will I be hungry? Who will feed me? Will I be cold? Will my family miss me?" The boy got a confused look on his face and said, "Huh? I don't want to play this game anymore."

The first child was a non-player. He needed help learning how to interact with the materials in his environment.

The second child only knew how to play by imitating what he had seen on television. His play was not imaginative and required little or no thinking ability. This is non-productive play. Breaking the television script is the first intervention step.

Most children will learn naturally through play. Some will need adults to show them how to play. Others will need further professional intervention.

The benefits of play are well established in research literature. Children who are good players are better learners and are better able to regulate their behaviors. Children who are good players are less likely to become criminals as adults (Frost, 1998; Brown, 2006).

Professional Referrals

Chapter two contains more information on simple intervention strategies. If these strategies do not work, the child should be referred to one or more of the following for further evaluation.

- Play Therapist
- Occupational Therapist for sensory integration evaluation
- Child Psychologist
- Child Psychiatrist

Developmental Delays and Other Medical Conditions

There are a number of conditions, beyond the scope of this book, which can affect growth and development. Any condition that interferes with a child's ability to interact with adults and materials in the environment can be a potential problem. Children who do not feel well, for whatever reason, may not feel like playing. Adult-child interactions can be affected when a child has unresolved pain. It is essential that health needs are met.

When Further Assistance is Needed

Determining whether a child needs a professional evaluation and where to begin can be difficult. Concerns may involve multiple issues which require referrals to various professionals.

Federal law requires local school districts to offer free Child Find screenings to preschoolers, when requested by a parent. A Child Find Assessment often includes hearing and vision screenings, speech/language testing, gross motor and fine motor assessment, as well as a screening for developmental delays. Some school districts offer therapy services and free preschool for those who meet eligibility guidelines. Requests for screenings can be made to the local school district's Child Find Coordinator.

Simple classroom observation tools are available for early childhood teachers. For more information, check with the early childhood coordinator at your local school district or your local child care resource and referral agency.

The Ages & Stages Questionnaires is an observation checklist for various ages and stages of development. This simple tool is easy for parents to use. Some medical offices and early childhood programs provide these forms for parents who use their services.

A number of internet websites offer information that can be beneficial in discussing concerns with professionals. The American Academy of Pediatrics and other professional organizations include information for parents on their websites

The following chart offers a brief overview of common concerns and where to begin searching for assistance. Symptoms will vary with individual children. Refer to Chapter 3 for typical development.

Concerns	Some common symptoms	Who Can Help
Abuse or Neglect	• Physical marks on body • Unclean appearance • Steals or hoards food • Child replays abuse through play	• Law enforcement • Pediatrician • Child Advocacy Centers
Attention Deficit Hyperactivity Disorder (ADHD)	• Difficulty concentrating • Possible hyperactivity • Impulsive behaviors	• Pediatrician • Child Psychologist • Child Psychiatrist
Delay in Large Motor Development	• Delays in rolling over, sitting, standing, walking, running, skipping, climbing	• Pediatrician • Child Find • Occupational Therapist • Physical Therapist
Delay in Small Motor Development	• Delays in eating with utensils, coloring, play with small toys, self-dressing and undressing	• Pediatrician • Child Find • Occupational Therapist
Food Allergies or Sensitivities	• Rash and/or upset stomach • Difficulty breathing • Dark circles under eyes • Difficulty concentrating	• Pediatric Allergist • Registered Dietitian or Nutritionist • Food Allergy Network
Gifted Children	• Easily frustrated and bored • Consider themselves equal to adults • Need to see big picture	• School Psychologist • Child Psychologist • Teacher for Gifted

Concerns	Some common symptoms	Who Can Help
Speech and Hearing	• Responds inconsistently to verbal instructions • Does not talk by 18 months • Does not use two-word sentences by age two • Does not use three-word sentences by age three	• Child Find • Speech Pathologist • Audiologist (Request tests for speech AND hearing.)
Sensory Processing (Symptoms vary according to specific senses involved)	• Delays in motor skills • Difficulty focusing eyes • Hears, but doesn't respond • Refuses to play when undeveloped senses are involved • Difficulty maintaining eye contact • Sensitive to noise and lights	• Occupational Therapist • Autism Specialist
Social-Emotional	• Resists being pick-up or held • Emotional disconnect • Eyes look glazed • Difficulty making and maintaining eye-contact • Difficulty playing • Extreme aggression • Abusive toward people and/or animals	• Licensed Professional Counselor • Child Psychologist • Child Psychiatrist • Play Therapist

CONCLUSION

Putting It All Together

The benefits of play and play-based learning, positive relationships, and healthy lifestyles are well documented in research literature. We know that sensory experiences in the early years of life form brain connections which are the foundation for lifelong learning and relationships. We also know that toxic stress and lack of sensory experiences can interfere with brain development.

Yet, as a society, our actions seldom follow the research. We expect children to be seen, but not heard. We limit outside play, music, art, and adult-child time. These have, too often, been replaced by more sitting, at school and at home. Many children receive more interaction from television and video games than from the adults in their lives.

It is time to bring back play. Children need playful interactions with adults and other children. They need to swing, rock, ride merry-go-rounds and climb. They need calmer environments, which support learning and development.

If you are a parent or teacher, find ways to calm your own stress, so you can better support the children in your lives. If you have unresolved issues from your own childhood, find help to resolve them, so you don't replay them as you interact with children. Be attuned to the needs of the children in your care.

If you are a policymaker, school administrator or business manager, consider how your decisions affect children and their families. Parents do not parent their children in isolation. Parenting is affected by demands of the broader community, such as working hours and school expectations.

More than any other generation, we know what children need to grow and develop into responsible adults. With this increased knowledge, comes increased responsibility. We can and must do better.

A child is a person who is going to carry on what you have started. He is going to sit where you are sitting and, when you are gone, attend to those things which you think are important. You may adopt all the policies you please, but how they will be carried out depends on him. He will assume control of your cities, states and nations. He is going to move in and take over your churches, schools, universities and corporations. All your books are going to be judged, praised or condemned by him. The fate of humanity is in his hands, so it might be well to pay him some attention.

—AUTHOR UNKNOWN*

*Credit for this quote is often attributed to Abraham Lincoln. However, research by the Lincoln Presidential Library was unable to confirm it. Therefore, the author remains unknown.

References

ADDitude, An ADHD Med Without Side Effects (2008, February 18). Retrieved April 4, 2009 from http://www.additudemag.com/adhd/article/print/3142.html

Allen, E. & Marotz, L. (1994) *Developmental Profiles: Pre-Birth through Eight.* New York: Delmar Publishers, Inc.

American Academy of Pediatrics (2006). *The Importance Of Play In Promoting Healthy Child Development and Maintaining Strong Parent-Child Bonds.* Retrieved October 2006 from www.aap.org

Blum, D. (1999, January/February). Attention Deficit. *Mother Jones,* p.58-61.

Boyer, E. L. (1991). *Ready to Learn: A Mandate for the Nation.* The Carnegie Foundation for the Advancement of Teaching. NJ: Princeton University Press.

Broberg, D., Broberg, K., McGuire, J. (2009). Policy Approaches to Offset Childhood Food Insecurity and Obesity. *Journal of Family and Consumer Sciences.* 101, 44-49.

Brown, S. (2006). *Play Deprived Life – Devastating Result.* Retrieved March 7, 2009 from www.nifplay.org/whitman.html

Carlsson-Paige, N. & Levin, D.E. (1990). *Who's Calling the Shots? How to Respond Effectively to Children's Fascination with War Play and War Toys.* Philadelphia, PA: New Society Publishers.

Carnegie Corporation of New York (1994) *Starting Points: Meeting the Needs of Our Youngest Children.* New York: Carnegie Corporation of New York.

Carnegie Corporation of New York (1996) *Years of Promise: A Comprehensive Learning Strategy for America's Children.*New York: Carnegie Corporation of New York.

Center for Disease Control (2008). *Nutrition and the Health of Young People.* Retrieved on April 23, 2009 from http://www.cdc.gov/healthyyouth/nutrition/facts.htm

Cooke, R. (2008, February 15). *Early childhood stress affects developingbrain. Retrieved on March 12, 2008 from* http://harvardscience.harvard.edu/print/20120

Doheny, K. (2007). *Food Additives May Make Kids Hyper.* Retrieved September 6, 2007 from http://children.webmd.com/news/20070906

Fiese, Barbara H. (2002). *A Review of 50 years of Research on Naturally Occurring Family Routines and Rituals: Cause for Celebration?* Journal of Family Psychology, (vol. 16, No. 4), pp. 381-390.

Frost, J.L. (1998, June). *Neuroscience, Play and Child Development.* Paper presented at IPA/USA Triennial National Conference (Longmont, CO, June 18-21, 1998). Published by Educational Resources Information Center (ERIC).

Gilliam, WS, *Prekindergarteners Left Behind: Explusion Rates in State Prekindergarten Programs* (Abbreviated as Foundation For Child Development Policy Brief Series No. 3, May 2005). Retrieved January 14, 2008 from www.fcd-us.org

Goleman, D. (1995). *Emotional Intelligence.* New York: Bantam Books.

Hannaford, C. (2005). *Smart Moves: Why Learning Is Not All In Your Head.* Salt Lake City, UT: Great River Books.

Hass, J. S., Lee, L.B., Kaplan, C.P., Sonneborn, D., Phillips, K.A., Liang, S. (2003). The Association of Race, Socioeconomic Status, and Health Insurance Status With the Prevalence of Overweight Among

Children and Adolescents. *American Journal of Public Health,* 93, 12. Retrieved April 21, 2009 from http://www.ajph.org/cgi/reprint/9?12/2/05.

Helfer, R.E. and Kempe, R.S. (1987). *The Battered Child.* Chicago: The University of Chicago Press.

Holick, M. (2006, June). *Vitamin D and Health: A D-Lightful Story.* Paper presented at Lillian Fountain Smith Conference for Nutrition Educators (Colorado State University, Fort Collins, CO, June 15-16, 2006).

Jensen, E. (1998). *Teaching with the Brain in Mind.* Alexandria,Virginia: Association for Supervision and CurriculumDevelopment.

Johnson, K. & Theberge, S. (2007). *Reducing Disparities Beginning in Early Childhood.* National Center for Children in Poverty. Retrieved April 21, 2009 from http://www.nccp.org/publications/pub_744.html

Kieffer,K. & Nicoll, J. (2005). *Violence in Video Games: A Review Of the Empirical Research.* (Abstract). Retrieved March 3, 2007 from www.apa.org.

Kluger, J. (2003, November 3). *Medicating Young Minds.* Time, p. 48.

Kranowitz, C.S. (2005). *The Out-of-Sync Child: Recognizing and Copingwith Sensory Processing Disorder.* NY: The Berkley Publishing Group.

Louv, R. (2005). *Last Child In the Woods: Saving Our Children From Nature-Deficit Disorder.* Chapel Hill, NC: Algonquin Books of Chapel Hill.

MacPherson, K. (2004, August 15). *Experts Concerned about Children's Creative Thinking.* Pittsburgh Post-Gazette. Retrieved from www.post-gazette.com.

McDevitt, T.M., & Ormrod, J. E. (2002). *Child Development and Education.* Upper Saddle River, NJ:

Merrill Prentice Hall. Medical News Today (2008, April 22*). Heart Tests Should Be Carried Out Before Treatment with Stimulant Drugs for Children with ADHD.* Retrieved from http://www.medicalnewstoday.com/articles/104904.php

Medline Plus (2008). *Medical Encyclopedia: Normal growth and development.* Retrieved April 21, 2009 from http://www.nlm.nih.gov/medlineplus/print/ency/article/002456.htm

Middlebrooks JS, Audage NC (2008). *The Effects of Childhood Stress on Health Across the Lifespan.* Atlanta (GA): Centers for Disease Control and Prevention, National Center for Injury Prevention and Control. Retrieved on March 12, 2008 from www.cdc.gov/injury

National Institute of Child Health & Human Development, *NIH News, March 26, 2007,* Retrieved March 26, 2007 from www.nih.gov

National Institutes of Health (2002, September 9). *Stress System Malfunction Could Lead to Serious, Life Threatening Disease* NIH Backgrounder. Retrieved on March 12, 2008 from www.nih.gov/news/pr/sep2002/nichd.09.htm

National Institutes of Mental Health Press Release (2007, November 12). *Brain Matures a Few Years Late in ADHD, But Follows Normal Pattern.* Retrieved from www.nimh.nih.gov/science-news/2007

National Parent Teacher Association (PTA) (2006, March 13).*Recess Is At Risk: New Campaign Comes to the Rescue.* National Parent Teacher Association. Retrieved August 2006. From www.pta.org/

National Scientific Council on the Developing Child (2004). *Children's emotional development is built into the architecture of their brains.* Working Paper No. 2. Retrieved August 15, 2008 from www.developingchild.net.

National Scientific Council on the Developing Child (2007). *The Timing and Quality of Early Experiences Combine to Shape Brain Architecture.* Working Paper No. 5. Retrieved August 15, 2008 from www.developingchild.net.

National Scientific Council on the Developing Child (2008). *Mental Health Problems in Early Childhood Can Impair Learning and Behavior for Life.* Working Paper No. 6. Retrieved January 24, 2009 fromwww.developingchild.net

National Sleep Foundation (2001). *Study Shows Connection Between Sleep and Childhood Injury.* Retrieved on March 12, 2008 from www.sleepforkids.org

National Sleep Foundation (2002). *Common Sleep Disorders Linked to ADHD.* Retrieved on March 12, 2008 from www.sleepforkids.org

National Sleep Foundation (2004). *The Sleep of America's Children.* Retrieved on March 12, 2008 from www.sleepforkids.org

National Sleep Foundation (2006). *Sleep-Wake Cycle: Its Physiology and Impact on Health.* Retrieved on August 27, 2008 fromwww.sleepfoundation.org

Perry, B.(1993). *Neurodevelopment and the psychophysiology of trauma II: Clinical work along the alarm-fear-terror continuum.* APSAC Advisor, 6:2, 1-20. Retrieved on March 12, 2008 from www.ChildTrauma.org

Perry, B. (2008, February 22). Training workshop. *Why Relational Health in Childhood Helps Create Healthy Communities – Applying Emerging Concepts in Neurobiology to Help Children, Families and Communities.* United Way of Weld County. Greeley, Colorado.

Pierson, J. (1994, September/October). *School Stress.* As We Grow, p.16.

Pierson, J. (1995, March/April). *The Value of Play.* As We Grow, p. 16.

Pierson, J. (1995, July/August). *Criteria for High Quality Infant/Toddler Child Care.* As We Grow, p. 6.

Pierson, J (1998). *Nutrition and Learning.* Colorado Early Childhood Journal, 1, 11-12.

Purdue News (June 1996). *Deficiency in omega-3 fatty acids tied to ADHD in boys.* Retrieved September 11, 1999 from http://purduenews.uns.purdue.edu/UNS/htm...html4ever/9608

Robinson, T., Borzekowski, D., Matheson, D., & Kraemer, H. (2007). Effects of Fast Food Branding on Young Children's Taste Preferences. *Archives of Pediatrics & Adolescent Medicine*, 161, 792-797.

Silverman, L. (2002). *UpSide-Down Brilliance: The Visual-Spatial Learner.* Denver, Colorado: DeLeon Publishing.

Somer, E. (1996). *Food & Mood.* New York: Henry Holt and Company.

Spiegel, A. (February 21, 2008). *Old-Fashioned Play Builds Serious Skills.* National Public Radio. Retrieved March 12, 2008 from www.npr.org.

Tyre, P. (2005, April 25). *Finding What Works.* Newsweek, p.54.

U.S. Food and Drug Administration Press Release (2004, October 15). *FDA Launches a Multi-Pronged Strategy to Strengthen Safeguards for Children Treated With Antidepressant Medications, FDA News, October 15, 2004.* Retrieved October 15, 2004 from www.fda.gov/

Viadero, D. (2008, February 13). Exercise Seen as Priming Pump for Students' Academic Strides. *Education Week* [online]. Retrieved April 4, 2009 from http://www.edweek.org/ew/articles/2008//02/13/23exercise_ep.h27.html?

Waring, M.E. & Lapane, K.L. (2008). Overweight in Children and Adolescents in Relation to Attention-Deficit/Hyperactivity Disorder: Results From a National Sample. *Pediatrics,* 2008, e1-e6. Retrieved April 21, 2009 from http://www.pediatrics.org/cgi/content/full/122/1/el

Weinhold, J.B., & Weinhold, B.K. (2007). *Healing Developmental Trauma: Processes for Advancing Human Evolution.* Swannanoa, NC: CICRCL Press.

Weinhold, B & Weinhold, J (2008a). *Breaking Free of the Co-dependency Trap.* Novato, California: New World Library.

Weinhold, J & Weinhold B (2008b). *The Flight from Intimacy – Healing Your Relationship of Counter-dependency – the Other Side of Co-dependency.* Novato, California: New World Library.

Wolfgang, C.H. (1977) *Helping Aggressive and Passive Preschoolers through Play.* Columbus, OH: Charles E. Merrill Publishing Company.

Acknowledgements

This book is the result of training and learning experiences throughout my career. My life has been touched by many colleagues, clients, students and parents. While it is impossible to list all of them, some deserve special acknowledgement.

I especially want to honor the memory of Charles Badley. As a psychologist, Charles was involved in the early research of this book before his untimely death. He provided valuable information about children's mental health, the psychology of color, Attention Deficit Hyperactivity Disorder (ADHD), and the effect of medication on behavior.

Janae Weinhold has been my friend, colleague and mentor for a number of years. Janae has patiently provided me with a counselor's perspective on children's social-emotional development, including intervention techniques.

A special thank you to my grandchildren who continue to teach me about today's children.

I also want to acknowledge those who provided valuable feedback that helped refine this book. Bette Matero, Carrie Dyster and Laura Yett provided a preschool perspective. Gail Kaliloa provided valuable insight from her experience as a preschool, elementary and reading teacher. Gail Adams and Kara Anderson provided an elementary teacher perspective. Greg Pierson provided a school administrative perspective. Jennifer Abbink provided information on Child Find Assessments.

Finally, I want to acknowledge those who were instrumental in making this book a reality, including Judith Briles, book shepherd, Kate Hawthorne Jeracki, copy editor, and Rebecca Finkel, book designer.

Index

LaVergne, TN USA
26 February 2010

174284LV00003B/1/P